ADVENTURES IN GIDEON

Kingdom Principles
&
Life Lessons My Dog
Taught Me

ঌ

ADVENTURES IN GIDEON

Kingdom Principles
&
Life Lessons My Dog Taught Me

&

by

Michele R. Brown

Unlock Publishing House
6715 Suitland Road
Suitland, MD 20746
www.unlockpublishinghouse.com

ISBN: 978-0-9903021-8-6

Unless otherwise indicated, all Scripture quotations are taken from the King James Version of the Bible.

Acknowledgments

Your first anything requires a village: first book, first child, first attempt to step out and do what you were born to do. It takes courage. It takes people reminding you that you can — by word, deed and investment. Those who by word have encouraged, coerced or otherwise forced this book from my heart and onto the page are too many to name but a few must be: Speedy Hicks, my personal progress conscience — Phyllis Anderson my BFF, whose wise and sweet words turn to a hiss if necessary; my sister-girl Dwanda Glenn Woodward who bores quickly of talk with no action and Patricia Brooks who taught me that I could do anything if I really wanted to — even run. A special shout out to my Mom and my Dad whose unfailing love pushes me no matter what the adventure — Marina Eva Harris Brown and Woodrow Wilson Brown are my inspiration for better or for worse. A special mention goes to my birth parents too who have by providence come into my life: Linda Clyburn and Kenneth Gladden.

Inspiration by deed: Angela Thornton my friend of 25+ years and first time author comes to mind — her book, *Unlocked: Keys To Godly Living* is an essential read for any sharer of the gospel. She introduced me to her publisher. Her leap of faith inspired me to do likewise; that's what friends are for as the song says. Debrena Jackson Gandy is my friend and mentor. I marvel at her transparency and willingness to share her life with so many. Twice she has successfully walked the path to book publishing; picked up by two outstanding publishing houses and has another book coming out very soon. I am honored that she wrote the Forward for my first effort. Her example lets me know that there will be others.

Inspiration by investment: I did a kickstarter.com campaign that was not successful — but here is the blessing. Just about every single investor that came through kickstarter.com agreed to support the project anyway. How awesome is that?

A heartfelt thank you to: Speedy Hicks, Olis Simmons, Kym Taylor, Lara Mendel, Reign Free Simpson, Debrena Jackson Gandy, Senobia Ellis, Antonio Lyons, Stephanie Hamlett, Steve Tillett, Angela Thornton, James Ballentine, Regena Thomas, Toni Michelle Jackson, and Gogi Hodder. Your investment in this work silenced every naysayer even my own voice at times.

True Foundation Ministries: Pastor Bruce & Velma Bagby and their family hold a special place in my heart concerning this work and my life in the Bay area.

A special word of gratitude to my spiritual father and ministry covering: Bishop Anthony L. Willis and First Lady Yvonne Willis. They have been a blessing in every way: by word, deed and investment. Shout out to my Lily of the Valley Christian Center family — there is NO PLACE like *The Lily*. *"Somebody gotta pray fo' da dogs!"*

Dedication

This book is dedicated to P. Misty Gideon, my first Weimaraner; my roommate and my inspiration. It is also dedicated to Grace, the Pitt Bull that I met because she had been tied to a pole in my church parking lot; mauled, half her jowl missing and wreaking of urine from the trauma of her attack. I did what I could to help her that fateful, third day of July, 2012 but it was ultimately too late for her. That encounter has forever changed my heart and my mind about the breed. I will always fight to end dog fighting rings and all the heinous activities and actions that surround it. It is an evil, murderous spirit that breeds terror and greater violence.

This book is the manifestation of a vow of obedience to God. I honor Him for His faithfulness and persistent boot in my back demanding my best and my trust in His sovereignty. I can still hear Him saying, "just keep walking." I am glad I did. To God be all the glory, great things He has done. I am the better for this work; I pray that you are too.

Contents

Foreword

As I sat down at my desk, intending to begin reading my dear friend Michele Brown's manuscript on my office computer, I was moved to listen to inspirational songs while I clicked through page after page and sipped on a latte. What happened next surprised me, shocked me and caught me off guard.

As I sat there reading her words that took me inside the extraordinary relationship she has with her Weimaraner Gideon, I could feel my heart literally expanding — no, exploding — open. Then add to it the spirit-filling songs pouring forth from my computer speakers as I read page after page; against the background of my favorite contemporary gospel songs and I was a boo-hooing, sobbing mess within minutes.

But instead of stemming the flow, I allowed the tears to continue streaming down my face as I absorbed word after word of her soul-enriching explanations of the profound expanse of God's love, the Kingdom message of Jesus Christ and the how the world was being changed, one person at a time, by her dog Gideon.

"The doors of my heart are flung wide open to receive," Michele shares early on in her book. *Oh yes*, and by reading this book, the doors of your heart will be flung open wide too. Whether or not you are a Christian, you can't help but be moved by her descriptions of the profound teachings of Jesus Christ and the life-lessons embedded in stories of the Bible that are brought alive through Gideon, and his interactions with others. For the first time, you might very well find yourself thinking to yourself, "I finally get it. I finally understand what that story or passage means."

It could be the chapter that illuminates one of "Pastor Gideon's" real-life teachings of forgiveness in action. Michele comments: "This is how real love operates. It does not remember an offense." In this instance, Gideon deepens her own ability to forgive, as he teaches her the "kind of forgiveness and reconciliation necessary to forgive those closest to you that injure you in the worst possible way." Her own capacity for unconditional love experiences a quantum leap while witnessing Gideon develop an endearing relationship over time with a young woman. "True repentance brings forth change," Gideon teaches her in yet another real-life situation that calls forth her own contrition.

It is remarkable to think that so much can be gained from a story about a woman and her dog — but Gideon is no ordinary dog — and Michele is certainly no ordinary woman. She's educated at the finest universities and colleges in the country; an illustrious career as a major player in politics around the country and an ordained minister — what a powerful combination. What Gideon taught Michele as a minister who is called, among other great things, to deliver Jesus' message of salvation, renewal and Kingdom living, he can teach you too. Whether the topic is faith, forgiveness, obedience, submission, non- judgment or unconditional love, it's been taught by Pastor Gideon. This is the nickname given by a neighbor who observes his ability to minister to people by tuning in to their pain or sorrow; raising his paw and placing it in their lap; changing a countenance with a compassionate look from his pale yellow eyes; or altering a mood with one of his infamous, enthusiastic tail-wagging greetings.

This book concludes with the best from her popular blog that started it all — the weekly blog that stirred hearts and encouraged its readers to go deeper in their walk with the Lord and their understanding of God's grace, mercy, and desire to draw us nearer to Him.

Maybe the greatest lesson that comes from these *Adventures* is one of the greatest messages brought by Jesus Christ — when we seek His Kingdom first; all the things we truly desire will be granted to us.

It is my hope that you will be touched, deeply within your spirit like I was — unexpectedly so... Most importantly, *be forever changed.*

Thank you, Gideon. Thank you, Michele for allowing your destinies as pet and owner to bless the world. Little did you know when God caused your lives to become intertwined that you would have a ministry *together.*

Debrena Jackson Gandy
National best-selling author
All the Joy You Can Stand
Sacred Pampering Principles
August 2013

☙

Introduction

This book was birthed out of my desire for a puppy, a canine companion. But it turned into a journey from passive, observational, internalized faith to a stronger, clearer, more vibrant and active faith in the power of God to do everything He promises, for anyone who dares to trust Him. *Adventures In Gideon* is the loveliest accident that has ever happened to me. I wanted a dog. I wanted someone to love me unconditionally in a strange city. In exchange, God gave me strength and self-confidence while reflecting my every weakness, short-coming, wart, gift and beauty through the watery blue eyes of a Weimaraner puppy. This fuzzy baby demanded that I be all that God requires of me privately — not just out in public where I had a title and a position. He demanded it at home where nobody but God could see my habits, fears, self-doubt and struggles.

My dog showed me that God was bigger than the dude I was reading about in the Bible or hearing about at church. He could handle everything I was facing, if I was willing to entrust it to Him. With every passing day, God used that little fuzzy wonder of mine to show His love, mercy and belief in me. Ultimately, I had no choice but to take God at His word and believe Him to take care of everything I was so desperate to change in me and in my life. I decided to partner with God to change my life and I am the better for it.

Adventures in Gideon tells our story — the first leg of the journey of Gideon and me — in hopes that it will encourage you to trust God, believe in yourself and love unconditionally. This journey is the most liberating process I have ever engaged. It is my prayer that by sharing these *adventures* you will find faith in God, a good laugh and the courage to live the life God has for you. My inspiration came from the most unlikely source, my puppy — so be on the lookout for yours.

Adventures In Gideon offers a basket of life lessons with simple truths embedded. It also shares Kingdom principles: life lessons with eternal truths embedded. Each truth is illustrated through adventures with my superhero of a dog, Gideon. Whether a life lesson or Kingdom principle, each episode reveals the love of God toward us. Gideon's actions, impulses and responses metaphorically reveal God's heart toward us or some wonderful facet of God's divine nature that each of us is called to embrace and apply to our own lives. Getting to know and love Gideon has been a beautiful reminder that God truly is love (1 John 4:8). It is the very nature of God, not just an attribute (1 John 4:16). Plant your foot on that truth and your life will begin to change.

PART ONE

A Word About The Kingdom

☙

A Word About The Kingdom

God's love for humanity compels Him to seek relationship with us and to seek a means of revealing Himself to us. The provision that God has made for true relationship with Him is through His Son, Jesus Christ. Jesus not only offers us access to God, but He also offers us access to the Kingdom of God/Kingdom of Heaven. Let's walk through Jesus' conversation with a Jewish ruler of His day to see exactly what these terms, *kingdom of God* and *kingdom of heaven* mean and how we are to apply them to our own lives today.

In the gospel of Matthew chapter 4, verse 17, Jesus' first utterance in public ministry is found: "repent for the kingdom of heaven is near." This cry for repentance is a call to a change of mindset. Repent here is not an emotional undoing before God; not just tears and sorrow; rather the Greek word *metanoia* which means to change your way of thinking. "Change your way of thinking because the Kingdom of heaven is at hand." Jesus personified this new way of being, doing, living and believing, having been sent to reintroduce this way of being into the culture of the times. Because of His assignment to reintroduce humanity to its original state of peace with God, delegated authority and dominion on earth, the religious leaders of the day wanted to kill Jesus. Jesus came offering them the Kingdom: a new mindset that would create a new lifestyle and way of walking in the earth.

Believing that Jesus is the Son of God; that He died so that we would not be eternally separated from God; and was raised from the dead three days later believing this (which is the meaning of being born again) offers the seeker of truth entrance into the Kingdom of God.

Once born again, the seeker of truth becomes a Believer (in Jesus Christ) and citizen of the Kingdom of God. This new system of belief ushers you into real relationship with God and grants you citizenship in the Kingdom — the realm of spiritual life, liberty and understanding that God originally intended for humanity. So begins the exciting adventure of living a Kingdom life: studying the word of God which is the Holy Bible, prayer, meditation and growing and maturing in your faith; not to mention new levels of personal success. This conversion experience opens your heart to the peace of God, the blessings of God and most of all, the manifestation of your destiny just as God intended it. This is what I discovered as I let go of religion (church rules and regulations that governed my outward appearance but did not address the inward state of my heart) and took hold of relationship with God through His Son, Jesus. My life has expanded and the doors of my heart are flung open wide to receive all that God has in store for my life.

The *Kingdom* in this book refers to the establishment of God's rule in humanity to live a life of power, authority and success in the natural and in the realm of the Spirit. This restored connection to God is maintained by the presence and power of the Holy Spirit at work in the heart, mind and life of a Kingdom citizen. Jesus is the principal example of what a Kingdom citizen looks like on earth.

All that He did as recorded in the gospels — healings, service, deliverance from demonic oppression, humility, power, love — we can do also if we believe.

PART TWO

The Adventure Begins

ॐ

Seek Ye First The Kingdom

Seek the Kingdom of God above all else, and live righteously, and he will give you everything you need.

Matthew 6:33 NLT

So don't be afraid, little flock. For it gives your Father great happiness to give you the Kingdom.

Luke 12:32 NLT

Kingdom Principle: The Kingdom of God must be our highest priority; Jesus gave us no other commission. *Rediscovering The Kingdom* by Dr. Myles Munroe

I came to Oakland in the fall of 2006 at the invitation of Mayor-elect Ronald V. Dellums and his wife, Cynthia. I had run into her at the Congressional Black Caucus Legislative Weekend in September and she coerced me (she would say *convinced* me) to come to Oakland to run their transition operation leading into the inaugural activities and to help set up shop in their new municipal home, City Hall. I declined until the Mayor came in and asked to speak to me directly. I had seen him in *JET Magazine* recently and was simply mesmerized. He came into the room with that 70's John Shaft swagger — so charming and so sweet. All he said was, "can I talk with you about my vision for the city of Oakland?" Even as I resisted, the hook sank deeper into my jaw as he talked about all that he wanted to do for the children of Oakland and for their families. I hadn't heard that kind of talk from an elected official since Jesse Jackson ran for President in '88.

Men and women of a certain generation, when they discuss the world, their leadership and place in it, do it in big broad strokes that capture your civic imagination and make you believe in them and in their vision. You can guess what happened. I drank the Kool-Aid and was soon landing in Oakland, California.

It wasn't long before I was offered the position of Deputy Chief of Staff and I relocated to the Left Coast, as we East Coasters call California. The people were different. The way they dressed was different. The way they thought was different. The food was different. The way they worshipped God was different. Even the way the gospel was presented was — you guessed it — different.

Being surrounded by so much difference was exhausting. The staff was a great team of people, but they were young and somewhat inexperienced. It was a lot of work, a lot of pressure, a lot of training, a lot of everything. It was all just different and a lot. I was bi- coastal for six months, commuting between Philly, the land of cheese steaks and the Liberty Bell, and Oakland, the land of... See's Candies? I mean really, what was Oakland really known for other than crack? That sounds awful, but as an outsider, I had not heard one positive thing about Oakland before I arrived.

One thing that can be said about my newest hometown is this: the citizens of Oakland are some die-hard folk. "Ride or die," as the kids say. They are going to go down with the ship when it comes to *The Town* (their nickname for Oakland). It is not a game.

They are so loyal, they can scare you. *Raider Nation* — scary. *East Bay pride* — scary. *I Hecka Love Oakland* — scary. Excessive, exponential love along with healthy doses of respect and loyalty to a city — not a person or a cause — a place. It took me some time to realize, Oakland is a cause. It is a vision. It is a reason.

While people get really serious when it comes to the *O*, I would need to live in the East Bay longer to have the fever as bad as some. East Bay pride is no joke. I was desperately homesick during the time I was getting to know my new hometown. The pressure of the new job, training a new staff to work together inside City Hall, and missing my mom and dad all weighed on me heavily. Like Paul in 2 Corinthians 12:8–9 when he was afflicted with a thorn in his flesh (a personal struggle), I went before the Lord and asked God to release me from this place so I could go back home — but to no avail. A pastor friend single-handedly prayed me through this transition. It was one of the most challenging journeys I have walked through as a believer in Jesus Christ.

Somewhere between snotting up my pillows and crying out to God in prayer, I realized He was not going to honor my petition to depart any time soon, so I might as well stop asking. Instead I started asking God for what I would need to stay in Oakland. What would make me comfortable? A dog! If I was going to live 3,000 miles from my daddy and my mom; my goddaughter Amber, my nieces and nephews — well, I needed a dog. I had been raised with them. My last dog died 10 years earlier. It was time. Oakland was definitely a dog town. This became my petition:

Lord, I want a dog.

My heavenly Father answered me swiftly in prayer. "Yes, you can have a dog..." But before I could say "YYYYAAAAY," He said, "for Christmas." "But it's July!" (*like He didn't know the date*). Again the word of the Lord came (where's the voice of Charlton Heston when you need it?), "You can have a dog for Christmas." I'm an intercessor, so I started interceding. I prayed and petitioned the Lord, and guess what He said: "You can have a dog for Christmas." I'm also a giver, so I thought: *I know what I'll do — I'll give an extra special offering at church. God will see my faithfulness and generosity and He'll accelerate His will for my life* (notice the deep spiritual spin I put on it). I went before the Lord in prayer again and guess what He said? "You can have a dog for Christmas." Same tone. Same message. I was considering a fast — but who does that unless absolutely necessary?

By now it was almost Columbus Day, so I could at least start looking; that would comfort me while I waited — maybe this was a faith walk. If I was going to name it and claim it, then I'd better start putting my faith to work and acting like it was already done. Notice how I put all my good charismatic Christian lingo to work? So much for that — the Lord, not being in the least bit impressed, ever so lovingly told me the same thing — "Christmas."

I was undeterred. I was on the internet every night after work checking out Weimaraner rescue sites. The breed choice deserves an explanation.

Once Upon A Time There Was Misty

I met my first Weimaraner, Misty, in New York City while I was in graduate school. He belonged to a university administrator that lived in my building. We (Misty and I) met in the lobby and it was love at first sight. He saw me and I saw him and it was over. We were fast friends and playmates. It was only after we'd turned the lobby into a dog park run that I noticed that Misty was attached to his mommy. By then it was settled, I loved him and he loved me.

We ran into each other almost thrice weekly and every time we greeted each other the same way: smiling, running, jumping, dancing, laughing and playing. After a while, his mommy invited me up to the apartment and then I was allowed to come by for intentional rather than coincidental time with my new friend. I would knock on the door and ask if Misty could come out and play. I was homesick and really missing my own dog who had passed away the year before. Coming to NYU was the perfect transition from the grief.

Misty's mommy was grateful because she had a busy household and didn't have time for the kind of play Misty wanted, so we were a match made in heaven. She lived on the Penthouse floor of our building in typical New York City style. There was one long hallway, which Misty and I turned into a dog run for two hours, twice a week. I'd gather the balls, pulls and treats and off we'd go — smiling, running, jumping, dancing, laughing and playing until Misty's mommy would come to the door and say it was time for Misty to settle down for bed. It was like the street lights coming on in the neighborhood. Nobody wanted to go home.

Because we were having so much fun, but Misty and I were comforted by our own little secret — we knew that we would see each other again real soon, and meanwhile we could communicate telepathically. Some days I would just "know" that he was in the lobby or heading out for a walk; and most of the time I was right.

Some days I would sit in the lobby and wait for him to come off the elevator so we could go play. Partially grateful for the break and partially succumbing to my pitiful, begging face, Misty's Mommy would relinquish him, giving strict instructions as she placed his leash in my hand. Then off we would go smiling, running, jumping, dancing, laughing and playing — my face turning to cheesy smiles and giggles. That was our play time together...

This was a shi-shi dog run with toys, a hose, water bowls — the works. It was so New York City upscale that it had a waiting list. "Members" needed a key to get in. You didn't just mosey up to the gate with your mutt and think you were going to have a free place to poop and scrub the asphalt — oh no, Ma'am. This was a Bleeker Street exclusive dog run — and it had community protocols. There will be none of this random visiting and moseying thank you. If you left your key and the folk on the other side of the fence didn't know you, they'd stand right there and not let you in the gate. When I first started going, I thought it was unbelievably rude — but as a "Member" I began to see the logic. There are few safe off-leash places for dog people and their pets to be a community. The dogs got along. The people got along (for the most part). Some strange dog that didn't know how to act or wasn't a part of the pack might disrupt our dog run time — either because of aggression or transgression. We refused to abide either. So you and your purebred whatever better keep it moving and poopie-scoopin', because you are not coming inside our "gated community" without an escort or a key — period.

Weekly, Misty and I joined our friends and I brought the *Sunday New York Times* thinking I was going to get a chance to read while he played with his furry friends, but it was not to be. Faithfully, he would come and knock the paper out of my hands and demand that I play with him. It began slowly at first: a tennis ball brought for me to throw so he could fetch. Then another, and another and another and before long — how could I read the paper when Misty was standing there all wide-eyed and eager. I gave in, and what a glorious indulgence! Besides, Misty turned his nose up at the other dogs. It was as if the dog park was for us to play in and the others were only allowed to watch the fun we had.

Occasionally Misty could visit overnight and we'd visit my friend Cheryl on the second floor. She had a cat named Malcolm. Very much like the iconic human that bore the same name, he was definitely a "by any means necessary" kind of cat. He and Misty had an understanding, and while I didn't cut the deal, the protocol was evident. There was an imaginary line in the middle of Cheryl's apartment that Misty better not cross or there would be hell (literally the absence of the presence of God) to pay.

One day Misty and I were strolling the neighborhood and we wandered two blocks east to Broadway — which this beautiful, completely agreeable dog refused to cross.

Through trial and error Misty made clear his "Broadway Aversion." No amount of treats, conversation or cajoling worked. No matter how I tried to distract; he knew Broadway and violently refused to cross it.

He was almost Ghandian: nonviolent but unrelenting. Ultimately, I stopped trying and we walked the other way. Again, 6th Ave, 7th Ave, all the way to the Hudson but not Broadway.

We lived in the same building for two glorious years. Time with Misty was fun and comforting. Just knowing that there was someone in that big city that really loved me, really knew me, and with whom I could play was the best cure for exams and fanatical professors.

In year three I didn't see Misty much. His family was traveling. I moved out of the building and Misty was beginning to summer in Connecticut with his grandmother. Misty was a typical New York City native. He too had a summer home. He usually just went for long weekends, but if the household was on the move, he'd spend a week or two away. I hated to see him go, but we had our telepathic communication. I'd always know when the car was pulling into the driveway with him returning from his summer home. What a grand reunion: once again the lobby was a dog run and we'd smile, run, jump, dance, laugh and play. It was pure joy.

As time went on, my visits with Misty were more intermittent. School work was increasing and I was accepted into the doctoral program. One day on my way to class I walked by the old building and ran into Misty's family in the lobby. "Where's Misty? I want to come upstairs and play before class — is that ok?" His mommy very casually said, "Oh Michele, Misty got hit by a car in Connecticut a few months ago and died." I lost it. I started screaming and running and jumping and dancing — but no laughing this time. His mommy ran behind me as I screamed, running in circles just like I would with Misty. I was inconsolable. It was a train wreck. I wasn't prepared for her news and she wasn't prepared for my outburst. Months had passed for her, but for me it was like he'd just been hit, laying there in front of me trying to catch his breath with me completely helpless to save him. I cried me a river over that dog.

I was so broke down I did not go to class that night. I went up to the second floor and sat on the mangy carpeted floor outside Cheryl's apartment, crying, until she came home. A passerby would have thought my mama died or something; I was so distraught. When I told Cheryl, she cried too — a true dog lover that one. We reminisced about Misty and all the fun we had had and I cried some more. I grieved him like a true friend.

I strolled by the dog run a few times. When my dog run community saw me "dogless," they knew what had happened. Nobody said anything. Each just gave me that OMG "dogless" look. Some looked away; others stared at the ground to avoid my gaze. They all knew what had happened. Then in typical New Yorker style one of them had the nerve to ask me about the disposition of the dog run key. Not "are you getting another dog?" Not "how are you makin' it?" This fool said, "Did she give you the key so we can contact someone on the waiting list?" Got to love New York. Always going to miss Misty.

Back to Begging

I knew that whenever I got another dog, it had to be a Weimaraner, in honor of my friend Misty. I knew by now that my begging was not working — but my internet search was comforting, so I kept it up. I located and engaged every rescue and animal shelter within a hundred mile radius of Oakland. I was on waitlists and e-blasts all over California. The more I talked to people, the more I realized that all the Weims in northern California were referred and handled by one breed rescue organization.

I applied online (*faith without works is dead*) for the Northern California Weimaraner Rescue and was turned down. I was told that my lifestyle and living arrangement (*an apartment dweller*) was not suitable for this kind of dog. Mind you, I met this breed in New York City where everyone lives in an apartment. Yet being the naïve soul that I can be, I decided to appeal the ruling. I wrote the Weim Rescue Czar (*my pet name for her*), explaining my plan and my living arrangements and how this dog was going to live better than some people I saw daily. I offered a lavish lifestyle plan of doggie daycare and any other special perks for my new "family member" (*dog lover lingo*). I even stalked the Rescue Czar for a while at public adoption fairs and special events. I'd go alone or sometimes with friends so that she could see how capable I was. See? No stupid Weim lover here, a lifelong dog lover; stable with a loving home. Why couldn't I offer that to one of the rescues? "No, and that's my final answer" was how the conversation ended via email.

I remained undeterred. *Lord, I want a dog.*

Late October. I started running across websites that had Weimaraner rescues that were mixed breed. No. Keep your game show toaster consolation prize. I want a full breed Weimaraner. That is what God said I could have, and by golly that's what I am going to get. Don't get me wrong; those Weim mixes were as cute as could be. They just weren't... Misty.

November. The weather is still warm. I cannot get used to the Bay area's Mediterranean climate. A hectic time at work, so I took a break for two weeks to enjoy some real winter weather back east. My research was paying off. I had been on so many websites that they started inviting me to register and now *they* are helping *me* find my dog. When the information circles began to converge, I knew I had saturated the market. I was running into the same people online and at events.

One unseasonably warm evening I was again petitioning God for my dog. But this time when I asked, I didn't hear anything. No reiterated answer, not anything. Just crickets... the sound of silence. I thought I'd better move on to some other topic. You ever asked your earthly parent something one too many times? There's that silence before something bad happens to you. For whatever reason, it was clear that my heavenly Father was not going to spend one more month discussing the disposition of my dog. It wasn't Christmas yet and that was all. End of discussion. You would think that a prayer "time-out" would have deterred me. I stopped raising the issue in prayer but I kept looking for my dog.

Rogue

I was out at a really upscale animal rescue event; a lightweight stalking expedition to try to plead my case face-to-face to the Weim Rescue Czar — when I met Rogue. She was the most beautiful American Bull Terrier I had ever seen. Mostly white with fawn markings, pink nose and the gentlest eyes. She was a rescue with a little skin problem that they were working on, but boy was she gorgeous and I don't even like female dogs. Rogue was so white, she was almost albino. Her skin was so sensitive she almost needed sun block to be outside. Yes, there is canine sun block.

I watched her as others came over to her crate. If she didn't want to be handled or engaged, she turned her back, showing her backside. Is that a strong enough message for you eager dog lover, that she's not interested? When I walked over with my friend, Rogue started smiling and running and jumping (sound familiar) and I lost it. We played and she looked at me and I looked at her and that was it.

However, here is the Kingdom lesson — it was not what God had promised. He promised me a Weimaraner puppy for Christmas. It was November and she was an American Bull Terrier.

Remember what happened to Abram when he didn't wait? The story is found in Genesis chapter 16. It's a page-turner. God promised Abram a son and in his impatience Abram allowed his wife to convince him to sleep with his Egyptian servant, Hagar. Hagar gave birth to Ishmael.

Rather than the child that God promised who was

Isaac coming forth unfettered, there are two nations that emerge from Abraham's loin instead of one. Those nations — the lineage of Ishmael (Arabs) and the lineage of Isaac (Jews) continue to war in the region we now call the Middle East. The moral of this story, mine and yours, is to wait on the Lord for exactly what He promised. God promises the Kingdom. When we don't wait, we create hindrances and blockages that can last a season, a lifetime or for generations to come.

I did not get Rogue that day because, while she was beautiful, she was true to her name. If you're an X- Men follower you know that Rogue was the name of the mutant with that shock of white hair that could zap the super powers and/or strength from anyone she touched. She couldn't even kiss her own boyfriend. When I saw Rogue I saw this cool, girl-dog superhero. Yet the definition of the word *Rogue* means vagrant, tramp, dishonest or worthless, scoundrel, scamp; mischievous; a horse inclined to shirk or misbehave; or an individual exhibiting a chance and unusual biological variation.

The same thing that happened to Abram would have happened to me for bringing into my home a mischievous scoundrel — but I wanted her anyway. Even though I watched her behave in a manner that was true to her name, I ignored the facts in favor of my fantasy. I was square-peg-round-holing it because I was not willing to wait on what God had promised. I would have brought home a full grown female American Bull Terrier (the taller version of a Pitt Bull) with a known, expensive medical condition and a turncoat disposition.

God says yes to our prayers and petitions, but then we are not willing to wait on the timing of the release of His perfect will. The delivery of exactly what we asked for, exactly what we need, and exactly what will propel us further into our destiny. Instead, in our haste we reach for a substitute, a reasonable facsimile, something less than heaven's best for us. Then we wonder why it doesn't work out. What we acquire on our own is not what God promised, leaving us to make the same hard choice as Abraham to correct the mistake. For Abraham that meant sending away a woman and a child he loved. It would have been the same for me. Rogue was already a rescue — she had already known her fair share of disappointments. My impatience would have added to *her* pain.

I wanted a dog. It didn't matter that it was the wrong breed, the wrong age, the wrong color, the wrong size and the wrong motive. I just wanted what I wanted when I wanted it. Selfish. Short-sighted. A grand invitation for trouble. Well, crisis averted. I left Rogue there that day saying that I would think about it and call them later. Die-hard knucklehead that I am, I did call but luckily Rogue was adopted by a loving family who could handle her. Bottom line: she was not mine. She was neither what I had asked for nor what God had promised.

After that real-life sermon about waiting for God and His promise, I couldn't go to any Weim websites in peace. For a few weeks I left it alone. Ok, a few days. However, when I went back to the internet, it was with a different mindset. I realized that I had almost blown my blessing because I was unwilling to wait. Now you know I had to apologize and tell God I was sorry.

I lay before the Lord one night wailing over the whole *Rogue Ultimatum* because I realized that I was wrong to behave so poorly.

Since then, I've learned that repentance is not just

being sorry. It's changing your mind and way of thinking, otherwise the behavior, attitude or opinion continues. True repentance brings forth change. Somewhere in my contrition session before the Lord, He made me get up.

Even He had grown weary of my shenanigans. So I wiped my face and went to my computer. But this time I was looking for what He had promised — and in my heart I was willing to wait on it. No longer preemptively searching for my dog, I was preparing to inherit the blessing He promised. That may sound like *Girl, all you did was switch gears — you were still looking for your dog.* Right, still looking for my dog — but my heart was different. I came off the Weim rescue site and did not bother the Weim Rescue Czar again. If they would not give me a dog, then obviously my blessing was not coming through them. I started looking at breeders and litters and the medical issues that are associated with Weims and how you care for them as puppies. What were their developmental stages like? Could I take pictures of my baby and sell them like William Wegman? I dove headlong into finding out about the dog God had promised me rather than *any* dog. I narrowed my search and waited on God.

On December 9, 2007 I was online at about 1:00 a.m. in the morning doing my usual search for photos and breeders. Most of the reputable breeders would not have a litter until the spring so I was asking myself how I was going to get a dog for Christmas. This is why you have to believe God: if those breeders would not have puppies until the spring, then they too were not going to be the vehicle for *my* blessing.

I was saying to God as the days of December ticked by that it was just about time for my present. I was getting really excited. I saw some litters and talked to some breeders. Weimaraners can be bred for hunting, for show or for family use. I wanted a dog of superior quality but I wanted him to be a family dog — although I liked the idea that I could show him competitively.

I have no idea what button I happened to push — I had been looking at websites routinely for about five months. I hit some button on the computer and up popped a website with what must have been every breed and every breeder nationwide. Clicking around in there I came upon Blue Ridge Weimaraners in Missouri — small breeders, family owned and operated. These people genuinely loved the breed and wanted to share that love with others. They guaranteed hips for two years. They sent along breed materials — books, cds, decals, authenticity papers, shot records and lineage information. They were thorough in terms of overall packaging. I needed everything they were offering and I had not run across another breeder who offered anything close. They wanted more than a purchase; they were offering the buyer a family member.

While Weimaraners are wonderful, it is no small feat to own one. Rather, it is a focused process of training, loving and disciplining them and then loving them some more. When I went on Blue Ridge Weimaraners' website, two of their championship dogs had just had a litter that would be ready to ship in two weeks. 9+14 = 23. The website had contact information, photos of the breeding facility, (USDA certified — another feature that I found important for such a small breeder) and chock full of solid information. They showed the parents of the new litter and pictures of the new puppies. When I clicked on Blue Ridge Weimaraners' website, I felt the spirit of the Lord... a calm excitement came over me. As I went through the site and made my way to the puppy photos, I was on the brink of tears because I knew that this was my day. The puppies were presented frontally, sitting on their haunches — which is a tricky balance at six weeks old. They are all big eyes and bellies so large that they rested on the floor between their hind legs. I scanned each photo carefully. I scrolled down till I came upon a big, fat Alfred Hitchcock look-alike.

And the Lord said clear as a bell:

"That's him. That's your baby."

"This one?"

"Yep, that one."

"I can have him? "

"Yes. You can have him."

Well, you know I lost it. I smiled. I ran. I jumped. I danced and laughed.

I said thank you to my heavenly Father for giving me exactly what I had asked for and, more importantly, exactly what He had for me — which was His best.

I'd already picked out a name: P. Misty Gideon. P was for Pepper, my very first dog as well as my most recently deceased dog. Misty whom I never wanted to forget. Gideon was what I'd decided to call my new puppy. Gideon, the unlikely warrior. I can't tell you where that came from, but that was the name I wanted for my new puppy — Gideon.

As I shared it with people, even before I found him, everyone loved it. My younger friends started calling him P. Giddy.

I clicked on my puppy's picture to select him. I called the breeder the next morning. Did I sleep at all that night? She and I talked and I shared my story about finding them online. She was amazed. I asked her a thousand and one questions, paid my money and on the 19th of December, P. Misty Gideon arrived at Oakland airport. Of course his new mommy was late picking him up — running through the airport like I lost my child. I asked around and found that they keep animals at the airline check in desk when they arrive. I carried my new bundle of joy to my car on a luggage cart, set him on the back seat and off we went. He was groggy from the trip and scared, but I scooped him up in my arms once we got home and held him all night long. His eyes were as big as saucers and his belly almost dragged the ground — my little porker. I loved him freely and completely because he was exactly what God had promised and exactly what I wanted.

We will always get God's best when we seek first the Kingdom: God's way of doing things, God's best for us delivered in His timing. For me, that meant being willing to stay in Oakland, the place of my employment and the place where my faith would be tested. It means being willing to wait on the Lord and follow His instructions to the letter. When we do, He will reward us with heaven's best. When we seek His Kingdom first, all the things we truly desire will be granted us.

Forgiveness Is A Currency of the Kingdom

Be kind and compassionate to one another, forgiving each other, just as in Christ God forgave you.

Ephesians 4:32 NKJV

Kingdom Principle: Practice Instant Forgiveness and Reconciliation

Most puppy books remind the new "parent" that a new puppy is like having a new baby. God knows that's the truth. They need food, water and shelter, care, protection, guidance and love and they will stop at nothing to get it including disrupt your entire day, weekend... life! And what a sweet disruption.

Gideon and I were adjusting nicely to each other and our new lifestyle of potty breaks, thrice daily feedings and limitless tender loving care. He was a furry baby and he required a lot of my time and attention. That was fine because he was providing me with what I needed too: someone to care for — something to love — some place to be myself. We were constant companions at home and in the car.

Prior to his arrival, being the bourgeois mommy that I was, I ransacked Pet Food Express and purchased his bedding, bowls and collar — all matching of course — it was khaki, fuzzy elegant, like a baby crib with the matching blanket set and bumper — or at least that's how I saw it. A circular bed so he would feel safe and cocooned — warm, fuzzy and totally encased in the best bedding his mommy could afford. He was not only going to be warm, but swaddled in style. Then I woke up.

When I brought Gideon home he was already too big for the puppy bed I bought. He looked like Marmaduke in a kiddy pool. Heading back to the store, I had a hard time finding the "couture" bedding in this new jumbo puppy size. What was available would ruin my color scheme (*I wanted it to match the living room*), which sent me on quite an adventure. Gideon of course didn't seem to mind, squatting in the top of the shopping cart, a wiggly little companion trying to get his sea legs in yet another form of transport. Inside of a week he had been in a crate, a car, an airplane, my truck and now he was negotiating a shopping cart. I padded the upper part of the cart with a portion of his bedding. I watched him try to make sense of this new reality, his eyes getting wider and wider with every aisle we cruised.

Even I was new to him. He'd wake up in the morning and look at me like "Lawd Jesus, where did *you* come from and where is my mommy?!" A look of shock followed by disappointment — so I held him and talked sweetly to help him feel better.

To find the right color and a certain style, we ventured through six Pet Marts-Villages-Expresses until I found the medium size version of my stylish couture puppy bed. We took it home along with a cart full of potty pads, poop scoop bags (*every dog park has these for free, but I didn't know that yet*) and doggie wipes (*a simple baby wipe will do*).

I set all this up in our new digs. Gideon loved it and laid right down. By the time I'd fetched a bottle of water from the fridge and come back into the room we now shared, he figured out that his bed had two parts a circular frame and an insert that he could chew. Those little razor teeth had already gone to work. I snatched him up and told him *No* — but he was still figuring out who I was, so how was he going to appreciate *No?* Instead of a verbal command, I distracted him from his destructive pursuit by playing with him which wore us both out.

As time went on I figured out that in order for Gideon to be happy, he needed stimulation — something to occupy his mind — something to play with. I went out in search of toys, a bunch of toys — toys that he played with until he figured out how to pulverize them. No cute scrunchy, squeezy toys for his little shark mouth. Nope, he needed tire rubber with a Goodyear stamp because his jaw was so strong. The harder the substance, the more Gideon was satisfied.

The other adjustment I had to adopt with my little pot-bellied wonder was his complete intoxication with food — which I discovered the hard way.

Gideon rode around in the car with me quite a bit. We had meals in the car. We took naps in the car. We made some great memories. He rode shotgun, ears flapping in the breeze, farting up my seats or trying to sit on me while I drove. I took him to an offsite meeting and my staff came out to meet the new addition to my family. He was hugged and petted and loved on. For my part, I was teased because I wasn't feeding Gideon enough; his ribs were showing, they claimed.

I said, my new mother hackles rising, that he is a hound; he is not supposed to be chubby. Besides, I feed him according to the serving instructions on the bag. They quickly retorted: "do *you* eat according to the bag portions?" Pearl clutch! I raced home and doubled Gideon's food portions and his ribs went away. OMG, was I starving my dog without knowing it? Bad mommy.

As I increased the food, I realized that Gideon really, really loved to eat. No, really. I mean really loved his food. So if I had something to do, the best thing was to leave him with something to chew on in the car. It was a perfect solution. Chewy foods or toys occupied his mind and kept his jaw busy. It was perfection — until that fateful day I left Gideon in the car and gave him a treat while I ran into my office to grab some documents. I came back to a train wreck. The bottom cushion of the driver's seat was demolished. My black cloth seat suddenly had polka dots — though not on the fabric. Physical holes had been punched into the seat. Gideon was six only months old.

Before I knew it, I had popped him and talked him through the spanking. You-know-better-than-this.

Now sit down! He was shocked and so was I. His eyes were wide and so were mine. I was so angry I could have farted a firecracker. I drove home and wouldn't look at him. My mind was racing. I could not believe Gideon had done such a thing. The more I scoured my brain for answers, the angrier I became. After all I had done for this dog! How could he be so insensitive? So ungrateful. So mischievous. So deviant. Every thought brought a harsher adjective to describe his inexplicable behavior.

Was I cut out for life with a puppy? After all that begging for a dog, now I was wondering if I could handle it. Have you ever gotten what you asked for and then wondered whether you could handle it? Did you even still want it? Would you ever be really ready for it?

Why had Gideon clawed my car seat?

I parked, snatched him out of the car, marched him through the lobby, put him in his area behind the baby gate in the kitchen — and walked away. His eyes were as big as half dollars. I was fuming and he was scared. He was in his room and I went to mine. I came out to get something and fussed at him some more. "Do you know how much a car seat costs? What were you thinking?" He was cowering in the corner because of the tone of my voice; getting smaller and smaller as I fussed and fussed and fussed about misbehaving and respecting my property and a list of "don't you ever do it again(s)." I went back to my room. It was probably the first night that Gideon and I were not going to be in the same room for nite-nite (yep, that's what I called it). We were both struggling. He whined a bit — but I was still too angry to be nice to him. On the inside, I was whining too. I missed having him in the room with me, but I had a point to make and I thought that making him suffer was the best way to make the point. Unfortunately, I was suffering too.

Every time he heard me move in my room, he whined. I tried to ignore it. I came out one last time in the wee hours of the morning.

There he was, only this time no whimpering or whining. He jumped right up when I entered the kitchen; ran up to me and began to joyfully lick my feet and jump on me. I was still unwilling to acknowledge him, so I grabbed my stuff and ran back into my room, confused by Gideon's loving response.

Finally, the Holy Spirit told me to go back out there and look at him. Gideon was jumping and smiling and dancing around again, happy to see me, like nothing had ever happened. He was waiting to embrace me, waiting for me to reciprocate. I was so convicted by his loving response, that I opened the baby gate, sat on the floor and an explosion of floppy ears, wet kisses, puppy gnawing and big paws erupted all over me. He licked my face so much I thought I lost a contact lens.

Clear as a bell, the Lord reminded me: This is how real love operates. It does not remember an offense. Love "is not irritable, and it keeps no record of being wronged" 1 Corinthians 13:5. Gideon had some understanding that he had done something wrong I'm sure, but his whining was not the whimper of contrition, it was a whimper of separation from me. He was alone in his pen, it was late and he did not want to be separated from me. He had no interest in my economic realities or my emotional gyrations. He was a fuzzy baby wanting his mommy. Separation was unacceptable.

The Lord was now fussing at me. All I could do was listen. God spoke so strongly and so soundly that all I could do was sit there on the floor at 3:00a.m. in the morning with Gideon climbing all over me.

God said to me, "Gideon's been trying to say sorry all night, and you would not let him." All I could do was cry. What kind of a mommy was I that I would be as cruel as to spank him *and* withhold my affection? At six months Gideon was already teaching me about motherhood, life, relationships — even about the Kingdom of God.

My puppy was teaching me about forgiveness. We are to be reconciled to each other, and we are to do it swiftly. We cannot ever withhold forgiveness because buried within it is the love of God — and we need both desperately. I was the one holding on to unforgiveness and offense — not puppy Gideon. He was ready to reconcile. I was the one that wasn't. I didn't want to forgive him. Holding the grudge felt better. That night on the floor in front of the washer and dryer, Gideon and I reconciled, and the Lord showed me once again a very important Kingdom lesson: forgiveness is a powerful act and it can and should be instant. All Gideon wanted was an opportunity to be forgiven. Isn't that what we all need? What if God was as unyielding as we can be? We would all be lost, separated and without hope.

Gideon's impulse was to reconcile; make it right; move on and love me again. Forgiveness is such a powerful act of spiritual maturity and grace that we must practice it early and often — like voting in Chicago. The moment I forgave Gideon and allowed him to love me again, was the moment I felt free to love him again too. It was the most liberating sensation. He was in my lap loving me. Who was I to deny him that or withhold affection from him? This is how we behave in our human relations; withholding affection, encouragement and support rather than reconciling ourselves in love.

Later in the month, I was talking to Gideon's doggy daycare handler and she told me, as she often does, an interesting dog fact: puppies have short attention spans, so disciplining them never need be longer than ten minutes. They can't remember the infraction much past that.

Lawd Jesus, dogs are biologically programmed to forgive; to not remember offense. They truly have the ministry of reconciliation — restoring right relationship and fellowship — and we should as well.

In the wee hours of the morning on the floor with my puppy, I learned that forgiveness is a currency of the Kingdom, a medium of exchange. It is how we must transact business and build relationships in the Kingdom of God. It was written a long time ago: forgive because we've been forgiven.

Epilogue

Months later, a member of my staff got in my car and asked me about the car seat. I fumed again. "Gideon chewed it and I STILL don't know why!" We went on to talk about some other things and when we got out of the car, the conversation ended. Later that day, while moving my car for me, he gave the car closer inspection. He reported back: "Hey boss, I think I know what happened to your seat. These aren't bite marks, they are claw marks. Look what I found between the seat and the drive shaft." Gideon's half eaten chew toy. "It had fallen between the seat and the driving column and he couldn't get to it. He was trying to dig up his chew toy. Typical puppy stuff. He didn't mean to tear your seat."

You ever seen a cartoon when the character does something stupid and the big black shoe heel comes over his face? That's how I felt. God was giving me a pop quiz and I still had the nerve to be "salty." I was instantly transported back to the floor of my apartment for another spanking in the spirit. I apologized again and told God I was no longer going to be so quick to jump to conclusions when I didn't know the whole story. Gideon was almost a year old and already he was teaching me lessons that far outweighed the inconvenience of potty training and a sleep schedule.

How many times have you said you forgive someone when in fact your forgiveness was temporary? Revisit the infraction and check your heart's response. Give what has been so freely given to you: forgiveness.

Dwell Together According to Knowledge Get Off My Bed!

Catch all the foxes, the little foxes before they ruin the vineyard of love, for the grapevines are blossoming!

Song of Solomon 2:15

Kingdom Principle: Submission to each other is a mirror of our submission to God.

Gideon was enjoying Just Pet Me (JPM), his doggy day school (*as my mother named it*). My work hours were so long I needed to know that my fuzzy baby would be safe, fed and learning. Gideon had been attending since he was eight weeks old. Now at six months, I was going to have to make a decision about his manhood. Would he reproduce the championship bloodline that he came from or would he be neutered? I was swamped with work and the pressure of having to make such a momentous decision was weighing me down. What was the right thing to do? Ruby, his handler at Just Pet Me, was pressuring me to decide by the time he was eight months old. It was a requirement to continue to attend. Like when your kid doesn't have all his vaccinations before he returns to school, Gideon was about to be expelled.

First reaction: negotiate. Why must we be so hasty? Can't he just grow up there nice 'n quiet like? He was such a sweet baby and such a handsome puppy — a face everyone even his playmates would love. Ruby explained that as Gideon entered his older puppy stage, he would biochemically start sending a signal that would cause the neutered dogs to attack him, rather than tolerate him as a puppy. An unaltered dog would compel the others to expel him from the group through some act of domination or violence. Long story short: his days were numbered.

What started out as cute was about to be problematic — and so it is with us, huh? Some of our habits and ways start out cute as children, maybe even young adults. But when we are adults, they are no longer acceptable behaviors, habits or ways of being. That's what Song of Solomon 2:15 is metaphorically referring to — when the writer declares "catch the small fox" he's talking about those small, seemingly insignificant areas of our lives that cause us to stumble. We call them: guilty pleasures, white lies, "can't-help-its, so-whats" and little secrets but God calls them small foxes that need to be captured; stumbling blocks — impediments to our maturation in Kingdom life and personal success.

Under duress I decided to have Gideon neutered. Here was the fist-ball-beat-em-all reason: if Gideon was not going to JPM, where would he go during the day at eight months old? He could not be alone all day. I had already tried having him in the car and popping down on breaks to feed, walk and cuddle with him. It was exhausting. He was accustomed to JPM and the schedule he was on — breakfast, playtime, snacks, feeding, nap time, play time and then dinner, a brief nap and play until Mommy picks me up. How could I interrupt all that? Replace it with what? All the places I called required a neutered dog — so this wasn't some conspiracy to induce me to neuter Gideon prematurely, it was a business protocol established by animal behaviorists who knew better.

Ok! I called his vet, Dr. Linn at Lake Veterinary Clinic in Oakland. She's the best.

My dogs have always picked their doctors. Gideon walked into the examination room and immediately begun to love on Dr. Linn. He licked her face, her hair, almost knocked her glasses off with his paw and tongue combo hug and she let him because all the while Gideon was playing, she was examining him. Brilliant. The only trauma was the thermometer in the butt and even that went smoothly. He loved her and she loved him. Heaven! So I took him in with me to discuss "the procedure." I was so bummed because part of me still wanted Gideon to sire a litter. In reality, when did I have time for that? I bombarded Dr. Linn with questions and when I was done, we scheduled the appointment two weeks hence.

The fateful Friday morning I dropped Gideon off, he was in a great mood. I had stalled another six weeks out of Ruby, so Gideon was eight and a half months old and getting bigger by the nanosecond. He was a little more aggressive and a little feistier, pushing back a little more at play time. It was time. I went off to work and asked them to call me when it was done. Dr. Linn called exactly 90 minutes after his drop-off. Everything had gone well and he was fine. I could pick him up any time. He was groggy and needed to sleep off anesthesia and I had work to do. By the time we were both ready, it would be fine to take him home. I arrived at 6:00pm to pick up my baby. By then he'd eaten his dinner and was feeling fine. Certain movements reminded him of his "procedure" and he yelped, but he was genuinely in a good mood.

I brought his cushy bed to transport him. When we reached home, I put him in a small shopping cart and we ever so gently went upstairs to our apartment.

Gideon rested quietly in his bed while I made dinner. We both dozed off. When I woke up, I put him in the kitchen in his cushy bed where he'd been sleeping. He whimpered a small protest but that was nothing new — he would fall back to sleep and all would be well. I changed for bed and could hear the whimper becoming a siren. I went to the kitchen. Turned on the light and the siren ceased. I looked at him, and he looked at me with refugee eyes. I sat down for a bit with him. When he fell asleep, I left. I settled into my bed and just as I was about to hit deep sleep, the siren started with renewed fervor. I was SO sleepy, but I didn't want it to wake my neighbors, so I put him in my room on the floor thinking he would be fine. I lifted him ever so gently and carried him to where he could see me, leaving the night light on (for both of us). I lay in my bed facing him. Problem solved. I turned off the overhead light and crossed my fingers.

It took almost twenty minutes before the whimpering began in earnest and the siren was not far behind. "Whus da matter mommy's boy?" I put on my robe, and got down on the floor with the fuzzy baby in his bed. So now I'm laying on my side wrapping myself around the brand new puppy bed, rocking and cajoling a puppy to sleep... fa real? Finally we both fell asleep. Now I can get back in my bed. I start my ease-back from the doggy bed, sliding my arm and rolling my hips away, then slinking my way onto my bed, aching hip and all. Just as my head hit the pillow... whimpering.

I looked down lovingly to comfort Gideon, while preparing to smother him with a pillow! I remembered Roseanne Barr's comment on the *Roseanne Show*, when her middle daughter was getting on her nerves, about mothers in the wild eating their young. Though I had not given birth to Gideon, I had paid a handsome sum and was about to forfeit my investment.

Without an option, I had a bright idea: put him and his bed on the end of my bed. We could both rest comfortably. Problem solved! That was a year ago. Gideon outgrew his bed quickly and refused, after his recovery, to return to the floor. Once he outgrew his bed, he had no problem adopting mine.

Months passed. I was lazy about disciplining him and he was happy to sleep with his Mommy. Gideon, I came to discover, comes from a breed of dogs that are truly creatures of comfort. As the dog magazines warned, if you have one of these breeds, you need a bigger sofa and a bigger bed. Two guys at the dog park confirmed this mystery in our breed-related chat. "Whatever you do, don't let him get in your bed — you'll never get him out!" "Oh, ok. Thanks for the advice." I was too embarrassed to say he'd been my roommate for almost a year! I came home one day and Gideon was not only on the bed, he was in it! Covers pulled up, head on pillow, same sleep position as mine. OMG.

Well the truth was I liked playing with Gideon. I read my books and magazines and he jumped on an off the bed trying to get my attention. He *and* I (guilty as charged) had turned my bed into a play space rather than my rest space and that had to change.

A year earlier I had gone home to visit a friend in

D.C. and had teased her because she let her two small dogs sleep with her. I had all kinds of prophetic things to say about how her husband could never show up because the dogs were occupying his space (*deep, right?*). During this latest visit she said out of the clear blue, "You have a dog now, right?"

"Yeah."

"Where does he sleep?"

I couldn't say a word.

She cleaned my clock: "You had AAAAAALL THAT to say about me and my dogs and here you got Lassie in bed with you! Well, your husband ain't comin' either til you get that dog out your bed!"

"Wow — why you gotta put the bad juju on me?"

My best friend went further: Gideon had to get out because my husband was coming, and I would be offended if *he* put him out. OK, OK, OK!

I came back from the trip determined to establish this new discipline. Each evening when Gideon would come to retire for the night to the corner of my bed, I would say *No*. A thousand times. Because of his cute antics or my own fatigue, eventually he won another round and would end up on the bed. A few mornings after I got back, during my devotional time the Lord challenged me. Get him out of your bed so your husband can get in it. WOW, really? Just like that? Straight — no chaser on this one. Ok, ok — piece a' cake.

That night I did the same thing: fussed and said "No" a thousand times and Gideon persisted with our evening "play and stay" ritual. He won for the next few months. Then another friend came over and saw Gideon on the bed during the day. He was so bold by now that every nap, every sleep experience was now on *our* bed. She challenged me as well. Three people and the Lord? Enough already! I really had to get with myself on this point.

What was really going on with me that I allowed this to continue? This was not Gideon's fault, it was mine. This was my "small fox" — this was my "little secret" that I could not get a handle on.

For many consecutive nights Gideon and I entered into a war of wills. I put some points on the board and he conceded to a leather wingback chair and ottoman in the corner of my room. Détente at last — for about a week. Then Gideon devised a new strategy. He would battle and feign defeat, retiring to the chair. At some point during the night when I was fast asleep, he would ease, one paw at a time, ever so gently, and ease, onto the bed. I'd wake up with him balled up in the small of my back or lying across my numbed feet. Other nights both of us, too battle weary for the bed, would fall asleep on the sofa and call a truce. This was becoming laughable — but just to me. My friends *and* God were putting the screws to me. Weeks turned to months. Gideon had even devised the I'm-sleeping-in-the-other-room-like-a-big-boy subterfuge. He'd go to sleep in the living room on the floor or the den on the loveseat. I would even check in on him to find him fast asleep. Later he'd slink into the bedroom, stare at me in my face to make sure I was asleep, and then ease onto the edge of the bed.

Ok, ok. It has to cease. "Michele, what is going on here?" I asked myself again. Ok, Ok, I like having my dog close to me! I miss the presence of a man in my bed and clearly Gideon's no substitute, but we have fun. And, since I'm not having *fun-fun* (*wink*), I can at least have fun! The Lord plucked me in the ear as I was meditating on all this and he commanded me to move Gideon out. Period. This was not a war of wills; this was my unwillingness to yield.

You will often have to give up something to receive what God has for you. In my case that meant: if you want a husband, you're going to have to prepare for him. That means clearing your sleeping quarters. Here's the other jewel. Gideon is a pack animal and that's how they sleep. He's also a Mommy's boy and the breed is very people focused, so his behavior is not unusual. He is also a creature of habit — and strong willed (*like his mommy*). He was going to fight for his own self-interest and I had to fight for mine. Not from a place of anger — I wasn't mad at him, I was amazed at his ingenuity. I was mad at myself for being unable to make the adjustment more swiftly. I needed Gideon as much as he needed me. I liked his heavy head on my legs at night. I liked reading my magazines while he threw his ball on the bed demanding we play fetch anyway. I had to hide my laughter the first time I watched him do his *Mission Impossible* slither onto the bed. But it was time for us to establish a boundary — because I was clear that if I didn't, God would. Time was running out. Gideon was almost 2 years old and this battle royale had begun at eight months. There, I said it.

I prayed for strength. The scripture in 1 Peter 3:7 about dwelling together according to knowledge had come to mind. While this scripture is usually quoted in terms of husbands and wives being in proper relationship to each other, I found that it has broader application in all relationships. The scripture suggests that each party must have a fundamental understanding of the other: respect differences and in every way, no matter what the frailty of the other, continue in love to model Christ in the relationship and in the shared home.

I had to show Gideon that I loved him, but make clear he could no longer sleep on my bed. I had to be loving, but firm — resolute in my decision if it was going to become the rule of the house. It wasn't Gideon being undisciplined, it was me.

Gideon knew long before I did that I was not ready to put him out of my room or off my bed — just like God knows when we are not ready, or are simply unwilling, to submit to Him. The other part of this lesson for me was obedience and faith. Honestly, when I drilled all the way down on it, I had to confess that I did not believe that God was going to honor my heart's cry for human companionship in the form of a husband. So why should I have to give up so basic a joy as playing with my dog on my bed? Good grief! Was everything becoming an obedience, faith and submission pop quiz? Well, the real answer is: Yes. It's all a pop quiz. Each trial, test and struggle is designed to test the integrity of our hearts. Do we love God enough to simply obey Him even when we don't understand? Even when it makes us uncomfortable? Even when we just plain don't want to? Obedience to God disturbs our free will and challenges us to submit. This test for me was designed to see if I love God enough to simply obey Him. Or would I continue to try to tantrum and eye-bat my way out of obedience? You know those looks we mastered as children... I could bat my eyes at my daddy like Minnie Mouse at Mickey and get whatever I wanted. So why not try it on God?

But God had already made it clear in other areas of my life that screaming for Him to pick me up was not going to happen. The floor was not on fire and while He was surely near, He was not picking me up out of my situation, fear or discomfort to save me this time.

Nor would there be any grand deliverance(s) — just quiet, private, deliberate obedience. It was now time to do as the hymn suggests: "trust and obey — for there's no other way, to be happy in Jesus, but to trust and obey."

Here's the object lesson: when my resolve shifted, so did Gideon's. When my *No* was real, Gideon's obedience to it was too. I'll not soon forget the first night I slept "Gideon-free" all night. At first I was shocked, then surprised, then proud of him. Later I was proud of me. I had done it — in the middle of the night when Gideon had slipped down the hall and into my room and begun his *Mission Impossible* paw-by-paw ascent, I awakened from a sound sleep and said *No*. Not an angry *No*; not an elevated voice or nastily toned *No*. Just lovingly firm and resolute *No*.

From that eventful night until now, Gideon has rarely slept in my bed — not gonna lie and say "never" but it is an event (*thunderstorm, gunfire, 4th of July fireworks*) rather than a way of life for us. He's tried to place a paw on the bed and look deeply into my eyes — like my version of Minnie Mouse's eye-batting — and I've simply held fast and told him *No* and he has moved on to curl up in the chair or to lay on his own bed — and it is well with both of us. His daddy/my husband is coming and Gideon is in his proper place. I had to return my bedroom to being a place of rest rather than an extension of the playroom that the rest of the house has become. That was three years ago. While my future husband and I have not yet met, I'm like Tom Bodette from *Motel 6* — leaving the light on for him — and keeping his place in the bed beside me clear.

Gideon's Foot Washing
&
The Law of Humility

You call me Teacher and Lord, and you are right, because that's what I am. And since I, your Lord and Teacher, have washed your feet, you ought to wash each other's feet. I have given you an example to follow. Do as I have done to you. I tell you the truth, slaves are not greater than their master. Nor is the messenger more important than the one who sends the message. Now that you know these things, God will bless you for doing them.

John 13:13–17 NLT

Kingdom Principle: Humility is the greatest virtue of a Kingdom citizen.

I grew up Baptist — of the dignified, it-don't-take-all-of-that school of church worship service. There were those in our fellowship who shouted and spoke in tongues, but for the most part our church was lively without erupting in the full blown Holy Ghost carnival like the Pentecostal church down the street that we affectionately called "the foot washers."

My black Baptist church was far more concerned with the literal, systematic understanding of the scriptures. Not to the exclusion of the Spirit, but we believed firmly in sound doctrine and a firm hold on the literal word of God. As a young person in the church, I participated in every Bible Bowl contest our Baptist Training Union (BTU) had — and our team always won because we were truly students of the scriptures. It was burned in my brain to study the word of God (the bible) and to seek answers for my life from its pages. It was not made clear in those days the role the Holy Spirit would play for me. His name was often referenced as our Helper, Comforter and Seal — but I did not understand the power His presence wielded in my own life. I saw Him show up in our communal worship experience, but I hadn't seen that same power in my personal life.

As my spiritual journey took me beyond my hometown, I experienced in college and in other cities where I lived, many different and wonderful worship experiences. Some were quiet and dignified. Some charismatic and free spirited. Others a complete circus: dancing, shouting, music, falling-out, and cloths tossed to cover those "slain in the spirit," which was quite a spectacle. One church even gave visitors a stick-figure brochure to explain what could be seen during the worship experience and the scriptural reference for the activity. It read: if you see this (stick-figure congregants with their hands lifted), this is an act of worship before the Lord. This brochure was informative for the new convert or visitor, assuring them that what they saw had scriptural basis and was not cultic or unusual — just new to them. I loved it.

One of my great spiritual adventures took me to a church that was not only spirit-filled in its communal worship, but also where they washed feet. A teaching was offered on humility and then the pastor washed the feet of the ministerial team and then together the leaders of the ministry washed the feet of the congregation. It was uncomfortable for all the obvious reasons: bare feet, bunions and corns; hammer toes and funny smells. Socks with holes in them and stockings with runs, all being revealed. Hilarious and humbling. Yet, the discomfort of revealing feet gave way to a solemnity and quietness of the soul that only the Holy Spirit can bring. As each pair of feet hit the water, tears began to flow. Hands lifted. Heads dropped in submission to God and to their leader. Rebellion in the pews was broken. Unforgiveness fled. Offense could not stay in our midst as feet were washed.

The power of God moved so mightily that the discomfort of bared feet and strange smells melted away and the Spirit of God took over. By the time our feet were dried, people were healed, delivered and truly set free. New attitudes, new insights, new life. I was amazed.

The first time I washed someone's feet I felt a compassion for them that I could not explain. It seemed I understood what they were going through — understood how and why they hurt. My only desire was God's best for them. I prayed differently. I felt more deeply about them and could love them even better. I wanted God to move on their behalf. The first time I had my feet washed, I was brought to a place of tears that was not sorrow. It was repentance — an overwhelmingly sincere need to seek the forgiveness of God and to restore right relationship. I wanted to be as close to Him as my faith would allow, and sin was hindering me. Something about that ritual broke the dam of my own pride and rebellion. By putting my feet in that water my arrogance was crushed, I was overwhelmed, enveloped in God's awesome love so that all I wanted of life was to love God back. To treat my neighbor right. Be a better parishioner. Love my church leaders and work even harder in God's church, my community and to be a better Kingdom citizen. There was definitely something to this foot washing experience.

As Gideon grew, his adventuresome spirit did too. When we went places, he wanted to explore. During his off leash dog park trips he was now venturing further and further away from me. His confidence was growing. So it is with us. We walk with God very closely at first and He deposits promises and His word, cultivating greatness in us. As our faith grows, He is able to send us out to encourage and minister to others. Whether a warm smile or a friendly hello, it's all an opportunity to share the love of God with someone.

As I had loved, trained and built Gideon's confidence, he too now felt confident to wander farther away to explore and experience all that the park had to offer and to engage all the doggies he would meet with confidence and curiosity.

As a result, when we returned home, we had to establish a ritual in the foyer of washing off and wiping down, so that my carpet did not resemble the dog park/ forest floor. It was also a way for me to check for ticks, fleas and any other "friends" he might have acquired outdoors that I wanted to stay outdoors where they would be happier. Light beige carpet had survived potty training fairly well; Gideon only had a few accidents. I was not going to add Stanley Steamer to my budget if I did not have to. So daily I wiped off Gideon's feet and wiped him down with baby wipes because I wasn't sure what he might have rolled in while off on one of his great adventures.

When I got Gideon, he was instantly adopted by a group of fun-loving women of great character and accomplishment — who identify themselves as Gideon's Aunties. One of his Aunties is a member of the oldest African American Pentecostal denomination in the world, the Church of God In Christ (COGIC) and one of their rituals of worship is foot-washing. When she kept Gideon while I was away, I demonstrated our little ritual so she could see what I meant about cleaning him and keeping my carpet clean. When I returned from my trip, she assured me that she had faithfully washed Gideon's feet. There was something about the way she said it that just made it funny. She said: "Yeah, Gideon is truly Pentecostal because he gets his feet washed daily! It doesn't get any more holy than that!"

She described their first foot-washing encounter in great detail. "We came in from the park and Gideon politely waited for me to take care of him. It was as if he knew he could not enter until he was properly groomed. But when I started cleaning him off, something just happened. You know I'm not a dog person. I love Gideon, but I'm not a dog lover, so all this was a bit much. But as I washed Gideon's feet, I just loved him even the more. I was so moved by the whole experience. I couldn't really explain it. Then I was on the phone with a friend telling her what happened, how my heart had opened up. She said, 'Oh, you washed the dog's feet' and together we said, 'It was the foot-washing!'"

How funny that foot-washing a dog had a similar impact to foot-washing a person! There's something about the act. It connects you to them in a whole new way. A deeper way. Whatever your level of affection, it deepens. And so it was with Gideon and his Auntie. After that particular visit, something shifted between them. She took him on runs around the lake. They continue to have a lovely relationship — and now all bathing and grooming is jokingly referred to as *foot washing.*

Pastor Gideon
&
The Ministry of Reconciliation

This means that anyone who belongs to Christ has become a new person. The old life is gone; a new life has begun. And all of this is a gift from God, who brought us back to Himself through Christ. And God has given us this task of reconciling people to Him. For God was in Christ, reconciling the world to Himself, no longer counting people's sins against them. And He gave us this wonderful message of reconciliation. So we are Christ's ambassadors; God is making his appeal through us. We speak for Christ when we plead, "come back to God!"

2 Corinthians 5:18–20 NLT

Kingdom Principle: We must be reconciled to God and each other.

Good Baptist girls are taught the word of God — make no mistake about it — sound biblical doctrine and lots of it. We live the life of the cultural black church: annual days (ushers, deaconess, men's, women's); dinners (fish, chicken, ribs); rehearsals (choir, plays, bible bowls) — all the institutional events that brought us together to put our religion on display. After all, our religious understanding includes the word of God *plus* activities and lots of them. Looking back, I think there were so many activities because we needed to be kept out of trouble. As a child, teen and even a young adult that made for me a community which I thoroughly enjoyed.

As an adult, however, it no longer rang true. Being Baptist wasn't really working for me by the time I hit graduate school. My friend at work was Pentecostal.

I really hadn't known anyone of that faith before. There was a small Pentecostal church down the street from my big, institutional, gold-standard Baptist church. We'd ride by their meager sanctuary and laugh because they'd still be in there having service at 3 p.m., having begun early that morning. We thought they were too animated and emotional in their worship. Yet, many aspects of our faith were similar — the dinners, annual days n' such, these activities that made any church a community of Believers. There was a depth of relationship that Pentecostalism seemed to offer that I had not encountered: an emotional connection to God. A longing for His presence and power and a demand placed on heaven for it that I had only seen in secret prayer meetings reserved for the "deep and super spiritual" subset of my Baptist church community. So when I saw all those elements of godliness manifest broadly in a church fellowship even within the men of the church, I was drawn to it like a moth to a flame. As anyone who's lived long enough to have life begin to happen to them — I needed God to be WAY bigger than my problems. Life was demanding of me a bigger faith. A stronger hope. A mightier God than the one of my childhood Baptist upbringing and I was determined to find Him.

My hunt for greater meaning took me to The House of the Lord Church in Brooklyn. I learned about the love of God. The power of real ministry, the kind of ministry that touches you and then resonates to impact generations of families within a community. I learned a lot about God and about my place in Him. I learned about reconciliation and forgiveness — not that hypothetical kind that you conjure up when some transgression has been manufactured. No, the kind of forgiveness and reconciliation necessary to visit a murderer in prison and host the funeral of his victim. That kind of forgiveness and reconciliation, necessary to forgive those closest to you that injure you in the worst possible way. They taught me that, but God was not finished with the lesson. I bounced between graduate school and my walks with Misty in New York, while keeping one foot in Washington, D.C. because in my travels I had met a man who would change my life forever — and forever settle the question of reconciliation.

Rev. Tom Skinner was a tall, strapping cat. Wide, ready smile. Warm, enveloping handshake — like sticking your hand in a catcher's mitt. He could eclipse the lighting in a room and then let out a laugh so disarming and gentle that you'd forget that he was tall and strong enough to snap your neck like a chicken — because it was the farthest thing from his mind. Tom was a gentle giant. He began most conversations with his cohort of young mentees this way: "Well, tell me, what's happening in your young life?" And so began his active listening to the endless babble of twenty-something tales of woe, confusion, mischief and promise. Our conversations were always filled with narcissistic rants that he crafted into dreams, destiny and purpose yet unborn. We didn't know it then, but Tom was making rich deposits in us just by gathering us together and listening.

Tom had founded something called the Leadership Retreat Family, a relatively private group of adult leaders that gathered for nothing more than the establishment and maintenance of good relationships. That was what he had in mind. A by-product was that much business was transacted as well. Tom's contention was this: if leaders knew each other — were in right relationship with each other — then everything else would flow from the fact that these adults in powerful positions would work together and support each other such that the agenda of the national African American community would be advanced, thereby advancing the Kingdom of God as well.

When there was trouble, as there often was, the firm foundation of solid relationship would be the basis for the necessary reconciliation. Tom saw that many things were broken in our national community because of the absence or brokenness of relationship. So much so that when momentous decisions needed to be made, they were sometimes perverted or miscarried because of broken relationship. Tom was a restorer of the breach. His ministry was like that of Jesus, the ministry of reconciliation. We needed, as the scriptures declared, to be reconciled to each other; and thereby we would be reconciling ourselves to God in the process. Tom believed that this was not only an essential teaching of the Kingdom, but a mandate for any Christian. He was never wanting for current examples of this.

He would say that relationships are so fragile, needed so much tending that we must take great care to be nurturing and supportive and attentive to them. We didn't understand it all, but we listened eagerly as the younger version of the adult Leadership Family group.

He inspired us to want to be the new and improved version — undeterred and unfazed by the vicissitudes of life and relationship that could cause such legendary fall-outs as the Hatfields and the McCoys. No matter what the infraction, Tom was always the one to reach out to the person and bring him/her back into relationship with the group, with the community, with himself/ herself and God. And he taught us to do the same. It was truly the love of God in action.

When a prominent politician was arrested, Tom visited him in jail; comforted his family and welcomed him home with a private homecoming celebration when the time came. Tom and I had innumerable conversations and debates about it. He was resolute — this man was a brother beloved and would be treated as such. All I could see was wasted genius and public embarrassment.

At twenty-something, I could not for the life of me understand why anyone would be so unnecessarily merciful — but Tom was steadfast — and he was right. He understood, as the Apostle Paul did, that someone left alone and out of the fellowship of family and true love too long is like a straggler in a herd who soon would be plucked off and destroyed by a predator. The enemy of their soul would come for them and they would be unable to defend themselves against their own vices or frailties. Not on Tom's watch! This man would have a soft place to land, would be surrounded by those that loved and respected him as a man, as a husband, as a father and as a soul. Period.

Tom taught us that reconciliation at its heart has a few divine qualities. Love. Empathy. Forgiveness. And a generosity of spirit that is irresistible.

Tom built community one love brick at a time, one understanding brick at a time, and one fully-embracing-you brick at a time. So he made all us youngsters come to greet this gentleman when he came home from prison. Come, welcome him back. Come, cook for him. Come, spend time with him. This politician is a cool dude. He was then and is now a brilliant man. One of the most talented political minds this nation has ever seen, drunk or sober. At the time, however, I was so undone by the request that I was pouting. Tom hemmed me in a corner and talked to me lovingly but sternly about my selfishness. (*Pearl clutch!*) He warned that I was going to need to be forgiven at some point in my life — and who would be there to do it but the ones for whom I had extended the same courtesy, honor and respect. So I showed up. I fried fish, washed greens, cleaned the kitchen, cooked food and made sweet tea all day. Our honored guest could not stop talking about how good everything tasted. His gratitude shamed me even more. Tom was right. He was and is a great man whatever his faults. Most importantly, he was Tom's friend and I respected that kind of love among men, among leaders, among brothers. Tom wanted us to love him the way he did. It was not a suggestion, it was a demand he was placing on us as his mentees, and so it is with God. Some things God offers to us as free gifts like salvation. Other things He commands: love and reconciliation are among them.

I learned through this politician's gratitude and Tom's freely extended hand, the power of reconciliation. Embedded in it I saw unconditional love.

Now what does this have to do with Gideon?

Gideon and I lived in a building that really had become community for us. As we came and went, we engaged our handful of neighbors and really bonded. We all took it very seriously, exchanging holiday cards, specialty foods, hugs and pleasantries. They watched Gideon grow from an eight-week old puppy, all paws and ears, into a doggy tall and strong — still all paws and ears. My neighbor nearby, Gladys was cordial to Gideon, but not a fan. She didn't want dog hair on her pants, and for heaven's sake she did not want him jumping on her. She was one of the few neighbors in the building that did not have a pet. I will admit that sometimes Gideon's enthusiasm was a little overwhelming, but everybody else loved him, so I figured she would come around too.

I came to observe that Gideon has a way of demanding that you love him, and so it was with my neighbor. Gideon is very empathic. It's a gift, really. He seems to sense the heart of a person and connect to it. So... though my neighbor Gladys would fuss about Gideon's hair on her pants and how he could absolutely not come into her home, she would faithfully pet him as he moved right past all her objections to give her a leaning hug and sit down in front of her until he was fully greeted.

I shared an incident with Gladys about an episode with my next door neighbor that I think accelerated permanent reconciliation between Gideon and Gladys and their coming to a permanent, mutual understanding and affection.

Gideon and my next door neighbor Lily love each other. I call her Gideon's girlfriend. She had come home one day truly distraught. Gideon was so moved by her sadness that he sat with her, placed his paw in her lap and refused to leave her side for the entire evening. He spent most of the night with her in her apartment, ate his dinner there and would have spent the night if that was necessary, he was that committed to making sure she was ok. When I finished sharing the story, Gladys started calling him "Pastor Gideon" because she said his actions toward our neighbor were pastoral. She was amazed at his concern for a human being — impressed even. She looked at Gideon and Gideon looked at her... The funny thing was not the name change from Gladys; the funny thing was Gideon's immediate response to it. Gideon answered to it perfectly from that day forward. It was as if in the recounting of this story, Gideon was embraced by Gladys as a valued member of the community, not just a reason to own a lint brush.

After that visit in the lobby of our building, her fussing ceased and the greetings grew warmer and warmer and longer and longer until there was usually a full blown sit down visit in the lobby between the two. I was invited to join in as well. As I suspected, she too joined the long list of people who loved and acknowledged Gideon as he moved through the building.

One day Gladys had a pastor friend visiting from Africa. She introduced Gideon as being a pastor too. Of course the visiting clergyman was confused, so she explained that in truth, this dog was doing the work of the ministry — he was full of compassion and love for everyone he encountered, no matter how cantankerous. He was a jewel in the building — a true blessing.

Gideon's loving care for the people in our building modeled the love of God: unconditional, consistent and ever available. Sometimes reconciliation isn't always about the forgiveness of an infraction, sometimes it's just an adjustment of worldview or perception. Gideon's behavior once again reminded me to do better in every area of my Kingdom walk. He reminded me of what Tom Skinner taught me twenty years ago: one day, you too will need the grace, mercy, love and forgiveness that you show others: make the deposit now, so you can make a withdrawal later when you will need it most. Tom was right. Life and time have allowed me the necessity to need all three: grace, mercy and forgiveness and while the law of reciprocity says you may not reap *where* you sow, you will surely receive a harvest. Now, I am daily reminded that reconciliation begins with me... thanks Tom, thanks Gideon.

A Sinful Woman Forgiven
How Gideon Loves (Jamie)

One of the Pharisees asked Jesus to have dinner with him, so Jesus went to his home and sat down to eat. When a certain immoral woman from that city heard he was eating there, she brought a beautiful alabaster jar filled with expensive perfume then she knelt behind him at his feet, weeping. Her tears fell on his feet, and she wiped them off with her hair. Then she kept kissing his feet and putting perfume on them.

When the Pharisee who had invited him saw this, he said to himself, "If this man were a prophet, he would know what kind of woman is touching him. She's a sinner!"

Then Jesus answered his thoughts. "Simon, I have something to say to you."

"Go ahead, Teacher," Simon replied.

Then Jesus told him this story. "A man loaned money to two people — 500 pieces of silver to one and 50 pieces of silver to the other. But neither of them could repay him, so he kindly forgave them both, canceling their debts. Who do you suppose loved him more after that?"

Simon answered, "I suppose the one for whom he cancelled the larger debt."

"That's right," Jesus said.

Then he turned to the woman and said to Simon, "Look at this woman kneeling here. When I entered your home, you didn't offer me water to wash the dust from my feet, but she has washed them with her tears and wiped them with her hair. You didn't greet me with a kiss, but from the time I first came in, she has not stopped kissing my feet. You neglected the courtesy of olive oil to anoint my head, but she has anointed my feet with rare perfume.

I tell you, her sins — and they are many — have been forgiven, so she has shown me much love. But a person who is forgiven little, shows only little love."

Then Jesus said to the woman, "Your sins are forgiven."

...And Jesus said to the woman, "Your faith has saved you; go in peace."

Luke 7:36–50 NLT

Kingdom Principle: Don't be so quick to judge.

Gideon loves Just Pet Me (JPM) Pet Spa, his home away from home since he was eight weeks old. His schedule had gone from daily to weekly so his visits now are even more precious. What I love about JPM is that he always returns to me tired — worn out from play, engagement with people and the excitement of being with his peers. His day at JPM was usually Sunday because they were such long ministry days for me. As we pulled in front of JPM one Sunday, a new face came to greet me. I was taken aback. Gideon was smitten.

As she approached the car, all I saw were tattoos flowing from the bottoms of her short sleeves and peeking through the top of her barely there t-shirt. The tattoos reached toward the nape of her neck engulfing most of the remaining visible skin. I was appalled. Gideon was overtaken with a look I'd never seen before.

She greeted me warmly. I offered a cool hello. She had treats to cajole Gideon from the car but none were needed — he practically leaped into her arms. She looked at him and he looked at her and from my rear view mirror, I could see them running through a field of daisies toward each other while violins played! *Unbelievable* was the word that came to mind as Gideon disembarked from the car. I was running to church. She smiled and wished me a good day and all I could do was smile. All the way to church I was talking to God about how hideous she looked with those tattoos and how she was such a "pretty girl" — why would she do that to herself? People just do anything these days, I reasoned. Her skin was so clean and clear and beautiful, she could be doing *Dove* commercials. Why would she ruin herself in this way? She probably called it adornment. I called it abomination.

Lawd Jesus. And why in heaven's name was Gideon so smitten by her? Good grief.

When I picked Gideon up that day, I inquired about her. *Who is she?* How has she come to this work? I basically wanted to know why she was chosen. I found out that she had all kinds of dog handling experience and really had a way with the animals. "A way" huh? Hmm.

Looking back on it, my conversation with God sounded much like the Pharisee in the parable of the sinner woman and the subsequent thoughts shared by Jesus' host captured at the opening of this adventure. Simon the Pharisee reasons that Jesus was the one who obviously didn't know who the woman was — trying to judge Jesus, while in fact, Jesus points out the true motive behind this religious leader's invitation to his home. It wasn't to host him as a house guest, it was to examine him. Self-righteousness, the bald-headed step-child of pride, is an enemy to Kingdom life and any form of spiritual maturity or faith. The presence of self-righteousness in our lives blinds us to our frailties and faults and causes us to sit as judges of others. We are called to be discerning, but not judging people. There is but one judge and He is God. Yet there I sat in my car all the way *to church* discussing with God *my* perceived waywardness of this young lady whom I did not know. The final insult was that Gideon seemed to LOVE her.

For the next few months, it seemed that no matter what time we arrived or came for pick up, Jamie the new handler greeted me at my car. I smiled but Gideon almost did cartwheels at the very sight of her. One day I had to go inside to handle some paperwork. She initiated a conversation.

"Hi Michele."

"Hello. Jamie right?"

"Yes. I'm the newest handler here... remember we met the other day..."

Yeah how could I forget with your billboard arms I sarcastically thought as I smiled in her face.

"Why yes!" came out of my mouth.

"Gideon is such a love. He follows me around all day. He actually got into a bit of a tussle today and had to be put in time out."

"Why?" My motherly hackles were ruffled.

"Well, because he got a little aggressive with another dog that approached me. And when that didn't work he tried to pee on me."

I went from consternation to laughter. "He what?"

"Yeah, he tried to pee on me because he is so protective and so insistent that I belong to him that he won't even allow the other trainer to feed him. He won't stay in any other play group but mine when I'm on duty — and you know there are always at least three of us here."

"OMG. Jamie if that weren't so embarrassing, it would be even funnier than it already is." I was floored. I looked over at Gideon who was dreamily gazing into Jamie's eyes while she recounted his day to me.

"Lawd Jesus, Gideon has a crush," I said half-heartedly.

"Yeah, looks like it," Jamie said. "Well, the feeling is mutual. He is the loveliest dog I've ever met. I have dogs of my own, but he is by far the greatest thing I've seen here and we get along just famously."

Even in my presence, Gideon never took his eyes off Jamie — he was truly "into her." He loved his mommy, but he *loved* Jamie. She went on to show me the tricks she'd taught him.

And as Gideon gave her his paw, rolled over, behaved perfectly on the lead and did a string of Lassie maneuvers, the spirit of the Lord convicted me. "You want the best for your dog and that is what he is getting from her — her very best. And he is reciprocating. He does not judge her. He discerns her heart toward him and he loves her."

You ever see the roadrunner cartoon when the coyote sets a trap and the roadrunner escapes, but the anvil falls from the cliff onto the coyote's head? Yeah, you get the picture. So as the anvil imprint rested on the top of my head, I kindly thanked Jamie for all the time she was taking with Gideon and said we'd see her later in the week. I scampered to the car like a rodent in daylight. I called to Gideon so we could leave, but in a split second he turned again to Jamie for one last hug and multiple kisses. She ended up joining us on the walk to the car because he just did not want to leave her side. I was so ashamed. Not only did I want the best possible care for my dog while I was away working, I also wanted him to be happy there. Gideon was safe, engaged and truly loving JPM. Simultaneously, I was convicted for my judgmental heart and silently condescending, self-righteous behavior. I wasn't rude to her, but I had decided on first impression that I did not like Jamie because of how she looked. As a black woman and heir of the Civil Rights Movement I knew better than that. I watched *Eyes On The Prize*. I heard Dr. King's *I Have A Dream* speech — "content of their character, not the color of their skin." And while I know Dr. King was addressing racial coloration — not dye selection for tattoos — the point was still the same. He dreamed and fought for us to have a world free of this kind of prejudice, a world that pre-judges people before we ever get a chance to know them.

As if this truth were not enough, there was the Kingdom life I had chosen as a Believer and a minister that was also being mocked by my prejudice. Jesus said it best in his conversation with Simon the Pharisee: the woman left forgiven of sin and Simon the religious leader big-shot was exposed as disingenuous and insincere. Urgh! I was acting like a Pharisee, while Gideon was modeling the love of God — ouch!

For the next few weeks I talked with Jamie — but

not because I engaged her. It was she who engaged me. I was too contrite now to do anything but listen and smile and encourage her. It was like the Holy Spirit had me in a headlock. Every time I saw her I was commanded to be kind, engaging, and to listen actively. And here's what I heard: Jamie was from the Midwest, had a wholesome upbringing. She was exploring her artistic leanings in school. She'd come out west with a friend for a change of scenery a year after high school. She was a little homesick, but really loved the Bay and was hopelessly devoted to Gideon. She went as far as to say that some days that was the best reason to show up for work, because she knew he'd be there. She said it was on those days that Gideon did not disappoint with his animated antics and effusive love for her.

Months passed and Jamie settled into the routine of JPM, now a seasoned member of the staff. We talked often about school and about what I was doing: freelance writing and ministry. She seemed fascinated by both.

Then she came to me and said that she had a big project for her class that somehow involved Gideon which she was anxious to share with me. When next we met, she read me a portion of a poem that included an homage to Gideon.

Do you know that even as I read it, Gideon sat in the lobby perfectly attentive just like he knew it was about him? Unbelievable. Jamie was a sweet girl, plain and simple and I was Shrek, an ogre (*I hide the green skin with make-up*).

Months later, Jamie announced that she was leaving town. She made a sweet request. Would I mind bringing Gideon in more so they could spend more time before she left? Maybe she could take him for a walk or something when he wasn't at JPM? Sure I said — let's work something out.

Jamie and Gideon illustrated the Kingdom Principles of love and humility. I had cast Jamie as the sinner woman in Jesus' parable whose story everybody knew and harshly judged. The narrative point I overlooked was that this woman had shown great courage and was the only one in the room who actually understood who Jesus really was: LOVE personified and worthy of worship even in the midst of her accusers. She offered Jesus her best and walked away forgiven. I on the other hand was behaving like Simon the Pharisee who needed forgiveness and didn't even know it.

I needed my dog and a perfect stranger to model it for me first and shame me into better behavior. My self-righteous condescension shut me off from being a portal of the love of God toward Jamie. I was too busy judging her and rehearsing with God my spiritual pedigree — all the things I don't do, all the ways I haven't sinned, all the reasons why I was somehow better than Jamie. The fact of the matter was I had failed God because my heart was not available to love her — which is the heart of kingdom citizenship and mindset. Love gives. Love enables God to use us to share kingdom teaching. Self-righteousness blinds us so we can no longer see how much we still need God.

All we see then is how much someone else does. Gideon saw Jamie's heart (*not her tattoos*) and freely gave of his own. That's Kingdom life at its best.

There Is Power, Power, Wonder Working Power In the Hug

Tax collectors and other notorious sinners often came to listen to Jesus teach.

This made the Pharisees and teachers of religious law complain that he was associating with such sinful people—even eating with them!

So Jesus told them this story:

"If a man has a hundred sheep and one of them gets lost, what will he do? Won't he leave the ninety-nine others in the wilderness and go to search for the one that is lost until he finds it?

And when he has found it, he will joyfully carry it home on his shoulders.

When he arrives, he will call together his friends and neighbors, saying, 'Rejoice with me because I have found my lost sheep.'

In the same way, there is more joy in heaven over one lost sinner who repents and returns to God than over ninety-nine others who are righteous and haven't strayed away!

Luke 15:1–7 NLT

Kingdom Principle: Never miss an opportunity to capture the heart of one.

The conversation *usually* begins like this: "What kind of dog is he? A Lab (Labrador Retriever)?" People say that because of Gideon's square head. Another voice will say "No, some kind of Greyhound." People say that because of his barrel chest and long legs. "Is he a

Great Dane?" This is just a poor guess because he's not nearly that big. "A Visla?" That breed is first cousin to the Weimaraner — German, smaller in frame, caramel colored but identical in temperament and body type. Finally when the guessing settles down I'll say,

"He's a Weimaraner."

And the standard response is: "Huh?"

"A Weim — a — raner," I say slower with some phonetic emphasis.

"Oh, do you know that guy that takes the pictures of the dogs that look like this?" someone else will say. "This dog should be photographed by him!"

"William Wegman is the photographer you're thinking of," I interject.

"Yeah, that's him. But this dog — there's something really special about him. He's so handsome, so calm."

Someone else will say, "Yeah, he's a real sweetheart. Look, so gentle too."

Then it happens. Gideon will find the one person in the circle of conversation who has not commented on his beautiful watery yellow eyes with the lingering specs of ocean blue that harken back to his puppy days. He'll find the one person that, for whatever reason, has not engaged him. In the midst of all that adoration, he will go and sit down in front of that one. If that doesn't work, he'll parade in front of him/her. If that doesn't seem to register, he will place his head under their dangling hand. Most times that will illicit the beginning of a pat on the head and a comment. "Oh hey, boy." Gideon will wag his tail and walk away to find the illusive favorite stick of the day. But if for some reason, the placement of his head under your hand does not engage you, he will give you a "hug."

A hug from Gideon is not the same as a human hug. That would be a full frontal assault, which is very poor canine behavior. Gideon hugs by leaning his full body weight on your legs and turning far enough around to look into your eyes. Something about this combination cat-dog behavior touches the heart of even the most distracted dog park visitor or unsuspecting conversant with Gideon's mommy. It has yielded the most endearing responses. Sometimes it elicits a story about a great Weimaraner the person once knew. Sometimes the person is jolted out of their distraction and hugs Gideon back, petting his head and rubbing on him and talking to him — which is all he really wants. Still other Gideon hugs have elicited tears and conversations about dogs that have recently passed away or stories of the last dog they owned that looked exactly like Gideon. It becomes clear their stand-offishness was not meant to be an offense; rather a defense. But how did Gideon know that?

As their story unfolds, Gideon sits there with them, eyeball to eyeball or haunch to hip taking it all in and comforting the speaker. His engagement of all kinds of people reminds me of what was said of Jesus and what was said by Jesus — that he would be a friend to the most unsavory members of the community (publicans and sinners.) Jesus was never concerned with what a person's surface condition or behavior was he always looked past that to their true need and spoke to it. That's what Gideon does with the people he meets. Clearly Gideon is not Jesus, but he sure does model

His behavior... better than I do sometimes. I probably wasn't giving much attention to the person who was not fully engaged — but that was the very one that Gideon honed in on. How many times have I missed an opportunity to show and share the love of God because I too was distracted?

As Kingdom citizens and ambassadors for Christ, we represent God in the earth at all times and must be ready and willing to give an account for our service. Gideon's service record was perfect; it was mine that needed... *attention.*

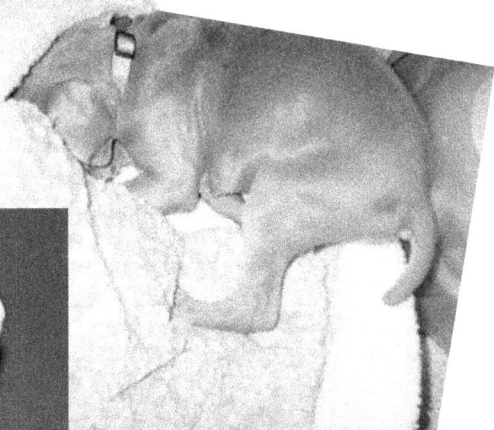

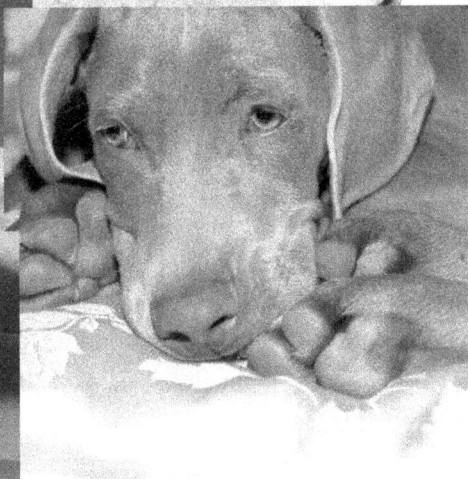

PART THREE

www.adventuresingideon.com

ക

Adventures In Gideon
Top Ten Blog Posts

Blogging has been an unexpected joy. I have my dear friend Anndretta to thank for the development of this site and the iron clad instruction that I had to prepare multiple posts before the site could go live. The process of being commanded to write consistently over a period of weeks prepared me for what would be my new life as a writer/blogger/author. Shout out to Dr. Nsenga Burton too because she was the one that introduced me to blogging and faithfully told me for years that I could do it. While this wasn't the subject matter either of us had in mind, it is nonetheless what has manifested.

At the request of many of my readers, the entries captured here are modified beyond what was written as a blog post to say a little more about each topic. I hope the remix is as good as the original. Thanks again to all my blog followers — you made me a writer and now an author.

In The Name of Longevity:
A Belly Rub In The Sun

I have been learning that it is better to praise Gideon's correct choices than too severely correct his poor choices. It's counterintuitive, but it's the truth. When I have a joyful, firm tone of voice with Gideon and give him instructions, he's still going to negotiate his response, but he's more likely to obey if I don't change my body language or manner of speech. Of course, the black mother in me wants to put my hand on my hip and fuss but I'm learning that it just doesn't work. Maybe it never did. Maybe it shouldn't.

Have you ever been in a relationship and had to change your mode of communication in the name of longevity — in order to honor the changes taking place within the relationship?

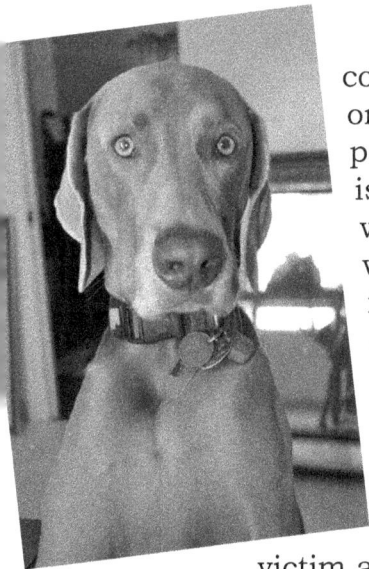

When I fussed, Gideon would cower and I would pick him up or run after him. Now, Gideon's pause after a command from me is not only a pause to consider what I've said, it's also a test of wills. Will Mommy burst into flames before I get into the car or will she wait patiently as I greet every person on the street and enter every merchant's doorway in my eternal hunt for treats on my way to the car? Some days I'm a burn victim and some days I pass the test — but what I'm learning is that in every relationship the communication has to be audited. You have to examine:

how you talk to people; how they talk to you; how you interact with people and how they respond to you — to make sure that the way you speak, honors how you feel about them and how you want them to feel when they leave your presence. National treasure and poet Maya Angelou says that people may not remember what you said, but they will remember how what you said made them feel.

Today I commanded Gideon to come to me and he refused. Right as I was about to raise my voice to him, he gave me this look like "think again" — it was a fleeting glance between he and I but it made me shift gears. I walked over to him and took him by the collar to pull him. He still wouldn't budge... like in a non-violent resistance kind of Ghandian way. I looked at him, he looked at me. So we started talking. I told him that we were about to go to the park. I told him we had to hurry. I told him that he can't cross the street by himself. Nothing. He just sat there staring at me. He lifted his nose in the air and let the warmth of the sun wash over him. I was so confused; I thought I'd try it too. Then I started pleading, "come on Gideon, we gotta go!" Nothing. He looked at me, I looked at him. Then I just stopped trying, and the moment I just released my "hurry," Gideon flopped over on the warm asphalt and rolled on his back begging me to rub his belly. It caught me completely off guard.

I thought: how many times have I been in conversation and was so focused on what I wanted; maybe even what I wanted for the other person, that I was oblivious to what they wanted... which in this case was a belly rub in the sun.

After I rubbed Gideon's belly, he got right up; shook himself, looked at me and gladly, obediently crossed the street. I was stunned... and dually warned... yanking on collars has now joined the list of unacceptable ways to communicate with Gideon. Wow, who's the owner again? As we went up the steps to my house, Gideon just gave me this look like, "see how easy that was?" Again I thought: how often have I missed a simple cue from a friend, co-worker, loved one or even a stranger who needed me to say or do something and because I was so distracted by what I wanted, I missed an opportunity to be a blessing; help or support to them?

Today, in the name of longevity, re-examine your communication with those in your life and general orbit and see if you're missing an opportunity to more fully communicate with them. They could want something as simple as a hug, a kiss, or a belly rub.

Be encouraged.

Reunion

As my vacation was coming to a close, even before the cruise ship I was sailing turned toward home, my heart began to turn... to remember how much I missed my family and friends... to begin to get excited about seeing Gideon having been away for a week. Yes, I was refreshed. Yes, I enjoyed myself immensely. Yes, I spent time clearing my head and my heart of all the debris that it can collect in the haste of life — but now it was just about time to come home.

I looked forward to being knocked over by 70 pounds of puppy love and excitement. I looked forward to wet doggy kisses that would dishevel my hair and wrinkle my clothes. I looked forward to momentarily smelling like a bag of old Frito corn chips because of the embrace of my doggy, Gideon.

I wondered how he had been. Did he get enough exercise? Did he have fun with his caretakers? Was he a good boy while I was away? Did he play with only his toys and share with his best friend Uncle JP? Did he come when called? A thousand questions began to run through my head as my heart turned toward home and the prospect of... our reunion.

My prayer for you today is that in your going and coming during this impending holiday season that each round of travel; each leg of your journey will end in a grand reunion with your loved ones both furry and human. How sweet it is to be missed. How sweet it is to be loved. The embrace of a loved one is nectar to the soul of a weary traveler.

And so it is in our journey through life, God longs to embrace us; to engage in the sweet reunion of fellowship. Quiet yourself long enough to commune with God and in the quietness of your own soul (mind, will, emotions) through prayer and meditation, reach for Him and I promise you, God will in turn, reach for you. What a sweet reunion!

Be encouraged.

Greetings

Today, as it unfolds every morning, Gideon greeted me with a big booty-breath yawn and some wet puppy kisses. He wiggles around in a circle like a puppy (Gideon is 4) and shakes his stump of a tail — then he circles closer and closer to me until he backs his butt up against my leg and beats me with his tail. He makes a funny growly, talky sound as he greets me, smiling and laughing and hugging.

I have a song I sing to him: Gooood Morning Giiiiiiiiideon! Goood Morning Giiiiiideon! No particular melody or tune... the beauty of it is he doesn't care about the tune or the words of the song as long as he hears his name. What he cares about is the greeting.

Gideon demands to be addressed when he wakes up. It is built into our relationship. He doesn't even care sometimes if I'm asleep. If he's awake, he wants me to acknowledge and love on him, even if that means I'm going to tell him to go back to bed or allow him to lay on mine (which is what usually happens).

As we enter this holiday season. Be mindful of the greeting. The opportunity for you to connect with another person. Begin in your own household. Ask someone how they're doing and then pause. Wait for a real answer. And if you don't get one — seek one out...

genuinely. When I greet Gideon, I examine him while I'm petting and playing — I'm checking that he's not in any way injured; in any level of distress and that all his basic physicality and emotions are intact. This is in fact, the purpose of a greeting isn't it? To engage the other person. To see how they're doing. The greeting is an invitation to engage, converse, embrace, listen, talk, and check-in. It's not a mindless drive-by expression exchanged so we can get to what we really want to say. Do not get so busy... so distracted by your own needs... so focused on someone or something else that you don't take the time to greet people — greet the day — greet yourself. Yes, that's right, yourself. Things that are not engaged daily are neglected and will wither; sometimes our neglect begins with ourselves.

We rush through our days bumping into things that bruise. Stumbling over words that injure us or others. Hitting where we should have hugged. Stopping when we should have pursued. Pursuing when everything in us said stop. Thus, greeting ourselves... stopping for a moment just to check in with us... examine our own hearts before we embark upon another day is yet another tool I want to offer you that Gideon has given me. The same way I examine him, I check my own head, heart and actions. Before I start the day I check to see if I'm alright. Do I need a nap? Comfort? Am I angry? Do I owe an apology somewhere in my world? Am I owed an apology somewhere in my world? A simple greeting — mine is usually Good Morning Father (yeah, I talk to God) and then after I address the source of all life, I say to myself whether audibly or not, the equivalent of: hey girl! As I prepare for my devotional time in the morning with God, while Gideon is still sleeping I greet myself and my day... with clarity, peace and the strength that only comes from God, I say... Good Day!

I want to challenge each of you to "the greeting." A pause in your earliest moments of the day to greet God, the lover of your soul and the source of your breath... then say hello to yourself... by then, your pooch will be awake and if not, it's time to greet your day. May the peace and love of God embrace each of your days this holiday season.

Be encouraged.

A Life Well-Lived

A number of great people died today. Rev. Fred Shuttlesworth, an 89 year old Civil Rights Movement legend that walked with Dr. Martin Luther King and was in Memphis when the four little girls were killed during the bombing of 16th Street Baptist church. A pastor friend lost his lovely wife way too soon. Steve Jobs, the co-founder of Apple also died today. Two of these three deaths made the New York Times and the world knew about it — one did not — but each is important and of eternal value.

Days like today beg the question:

What is the value of a life really?

Life is, in the words of the MasterCard campaign, priceless. Be reminded today to make each day count and to fill it with as much love as your heart can hold... as much laughter as your jaws can stand and as much joy as your arms can embrace... because life is short, wealth will not prolong it... the moments that populate your life truly are its fabric, its substance, its value.

Writing brings me joy. Pursuing my relationship with God brings me joy. My daddy's jack-o-lantern smile brings me joy. Gideon brings me joy and encouraging YOU brings me joy. What brings you joy? If you're not doing it, chasing it or becoming it, then you will not end up with "a life well-lived" and anything less than that is unacceptable. Start today. Commit to pursuing joy.

I captured a portion of Steve Jobs' commencement remarks to Stanford grads in 2005. His words are wise and instructive.

On Work...

"Work will fill a large part of your life and the only way to be truly satisfied is to do what you believe to be great work and the only way to do great work is to love what you do — if you haven't found it yet, keep looking and don't settle..."

On Death...

"No one wants to die. Even people who want to go to heaven don't want to die to get there and yet death is a destination we all share. No one has ever escaped it and that is as it should be — because death is very likely the single best invention of life — it is life's change agent — it clears out the old to make way for the new. Your time is limited so don't waste it living someone else's life. Don't be trapped by dogma — which is living with the results of other people's thinking. Don't let the noise of the opinions of others drown out your own inner voice. Most important, have the courage to follow your heart and intuition — they somehow already know what you truly want to become. Everything else is secondary."

Be encouraged.

Sinking...

I saw this image of Nicole Graham a few weeks ago and I could not shake the metaphor that came to mind...

This equestrian had been riding that same beach for 20 years without incident but on this fateful day, all that changed and she and her horse found themselves in neck high quicksand. What began as a good idea; something that seemed totally harmless; something that had been done a thousand times before was now threatening her life and the life of her 18 year old horse... in an instant.

This is what happens when sin enters our lives. Sin isn't a word I use often in my communication with you, but it is appropriate here. Sin, is the nature within us, a way of being that separates us from God. It is the will to do what we want rather than what God wants for us. It is an evil intention that can only be changed;

eternally altered by the love of God and real relationship with His Son, Jesus Christ.

There was something about the image of both of them completely covered in mud that I just could not shake. It reminded me of what I must have looked like when I came to God for help. I'd done my life my way for so long and it just wasn't working. Yes, I was successful. Yes, I had a good life. Yes, I had a great relationship, yet there was an emptiness that I could not explain. The emptiness was the absence of God from the journey which was my life. I was making my own decisions. I was creating my own opportunities. I was using what I thought was my own good judgment about what was best for me... and still this emptiness. Why wasn't I happy?

Why wasn't I *completely* fulfilled?

Because there is a place in us that only the presence of God can fill.

God loves us so much that His eternal desire is relationship with us and when a holy God seeks to love fallen, sinful mankind there has to be a mediator, a bridge to join the holy God and sinful mankind and that bridge was Jesus Christ. There is a consequence for sin; a price that has to be paid by someone and Jesus agreed to eternally pay the price for our sin — which means Jesus took on the penalty, weight and cost of every mistake, failure, fault, proclivity, wrong-doing and evil that we have *or will ever do* — so that we could be in eternal, peaceful and free relationship with a holy God.

Jesus stepped into the mud with us and would not leave us, just like Nicole would not leave her horse to die on that beach alone — neither would Jesus leave us to die in our situation. Jesus, the Son of God meets each of us right where we are — in the mud — in our sudden and unplanned mistakes, faults and failures and He says to us: I will not leave you. I will help you. I have always loved you and I have not changed my mind about you just because there's an issue, situation, circumstance or error. Together, we can do anything — you and me.

All we have to do is receive in our hearts the offer of a real relationship with God through His Son, Jesus Christ. Upon our acceptance of this free gift of love and relationship, Jesus comes into our hearts and begins the work of changing us from the inside out and making us into the best image of ourselves that we can be. He changes us and helps us become the authentic and originally planned version of ourselves — the person that God always intended us to be. Now begins the journey of really living. Really seeing life for what it is supposed to be — joyful, liberating, encouraging and infused with the love of God from beginning to end. It is this relationship with God; it is this acceptance of the free gift of His love and relationship that opens wide the door of our hearts and gains us entrance into a great life now and an even greater eternal life with God.

So no matter where we are on the journey called life, we may end up in some mud — suddenly — and need some help. I want you to know today that help is available. Help is on the way. This help is not temporary but eternal and that the love of God is all around you, ever available to you and waiting to help you. You do not have to walk through this life alone. You can walk with God in peace, power and joy. Receive the free gift of love and relationship with God through Jesus Christ and I promise you a real adventure.

There is a happy ending to the story. Astro the horse is rescued and so is Nicole... she was determined not to leave her horse's side, but to comfort and help him. Her love for him kept him alive. She risked a rising tide and her own injury and fatigue to save Astro. She did not think of herself, but of his needs.

So it is with God — it is His love for us that saves us and brings us into fellowship... Jesus took no thought for His own life when He died a gruesome death on a Roman cross so that we would never have to know the emptiness and pain of separation from God. So that emptiness that you feel no matter what you do; no matter where you go; no matter what you drink or smoke or who you sleep with can go away. Only God can fill the void. Only God can help by offering you the loving and eternal embrace of the God who has always and will always love you.

Be encouraged.

Loss. Renewal. Rebirth.

I'm learning that where there is the promise of great blessing, success, accomplishment, advancement; there is, as with the law of physics, the equal and opposite force of opposition to the blessing, success, accomplishment and advancement. In order to break the centrifugal force that surrounds your breakthrough to (fill in the blank), you are going to have to push through the opposition, break out of your difficulty and fight.

I just saw *Red Tails*, the George Lucas film about the legendary Tuskegee Airmen. This film along with so many others made me so proud of my cultural heritage and so inspired to do more with my life. I did not endure any of the institutional oppositions that these men faced. So what is my excuse for not doing more; going farther and completing my course with honor as these men did? None. I'm not facing real opposition, I'm facing myself and my ongoing distractions: people, places, things that I deem more important than the advancement of my own life. Well in 2012, this will not be my story. How about you?

I've been off the grid a bit due to a series of losses, renewals and rebirths. I lost a cousin, an uncle and the father of my best friend who was like a father to me. I have however renewed my faith in God's power to change me and any situation that comes my way. Finally, my creativity, courage and clarity have been reborn.

Decide today that there is nothing that can stand between you and your destiny. Let the love of God flow through you and lead you to victory. As the Tuskegee Airmen declare in *Red Tails*: "we fight, we fight, we fight!"

Be Encouraged.

More Than A Holiday
A Call To Action...
Remembering Dr. King

"I have decided to stick to love... hate is too great a burden to bear..."

"Darkness cannot drive out darkness: only light can do that. Hate cannot drive out hate: only love can do that."

"Love is the only force capable of transforming an enemy into a friend..."

"Everybody can be great... because anybody can serve. You don't have to have a college degree to serve. You don't have to make your subject and verb agree to serve. You only need a heart full of grace and a soul generated by love."

Excerpts from *A Testament of Hope: The Essential Writings and Speeches by Dr. Martin Luther King Jr.*

Today we remember the life, work, sacrifice and legacy of Dr. Martin Luther King. In his own words, he reminds each of us of the power of love, even the love of God.

This young Baptist preacher, seminarian and non-violent change agent knew that love remains the most powerful force in the earth. It has the power to changes us. Improve our condition. Expand our hearts and minds. Rekindle relationships. Make enemies friends. Shift systems and world views for the better.

Surely America is the better because Dr. King chose love as his strategy and tool for change.

The legacy of Dr. Martin Luther King reminds us that even love carries a burden and a price when we seek to reinforce it within our own lives and certainly within a culture. Dr. King paid with his life. So did Ghandi. So did Jesus. Two men he modeled his life after. In much smaller ways, we too will pay a price to model, show and share love. I have determined that it is nevertheless a price worth paying. What do you say?

As we share love, seek love and become portals for the flow of love in our own lives, remember Dr. King today and know that even your individual decision is an axe to the root of hatred and indifference in the world. Let the love of God be released in the earth today through you and I... even Gideon ☺

Be Encouraged.

Gratitude: Finding A Reason To Smile

While on vacation in St. Maarten I came across the cutest mutt walking along the town plaza. He was greeting people with his eyes and moving among the throngs of tourists and townspeople with such ease. His eyes were bright and his smile, wide. Then I noticed his slightly protruding ribs and hip bones and remembered Gideon. I was already missing him five days into my vacation, but seeing this lovely dog *really* made me miss him.

I was reminded of how fortunate I was to have Gideon and how fortunate Gideon was to have me. He knew that I would feed and care for him no matter where I was in the world — he would be taken care of. I knew that no matter where I was in the world, Gideon was missing his mommy. I wanted this doggy from halfway around the world to have the same opportunity.

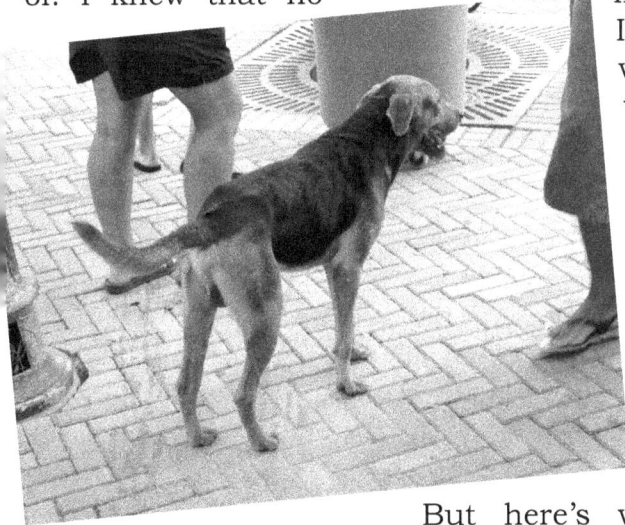

But here's what was so special about this doggy — his smile and demeanor never belied the fact that he was hungry or sickly. He was not focusing on his own condition. He was not aggressive or hostile — he was sweet and welcoming. Therein lies the lesson for us.

We have to find something to be grateful for every day. Some reason to give thanks. Some reason to smile rather than frown; to rejoice rather than complain. This island pup had every reason to be in a bad mood; to appear desperate and afraid but he was not. He was smiling. He was happy. He was expecting something good. I hope that we will do likewise in our lives... no matter what your situation in life, expect something good to come of it. Expect God to take your past mistakes, illnesses, distresses and problems and turn them into tales of victory... and until that day, be grateful and find a reason to smile.

Be encouraged.

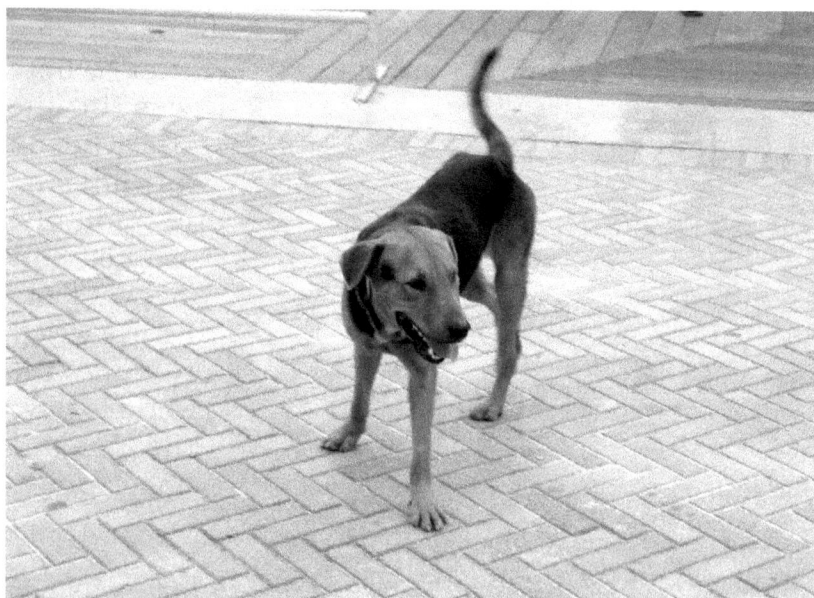

Rolling In Poop

Yesterday I took Gideon to Point Isabel near the Richmond, CA Marina. It was a treat really. Sundays are so hectic I don't get to take him on a long walk; he's usually consigned to the yard. On this particular Monday I really wanted to make it up to him; get some exercise and clear my own head.

I called my friend Peggy whose dog is best friends with Gideon, Uncle JP. We all piled into Peggy's car along with her partner and off to the dog park we went. Everything was going along just fine — we were laughing and catching up as the dogs ran and played and burned off lots of energy. Then almost from out of nowhere Gideon found a freshly laid pile of poop and rolled his hind parts in it! I was mortified. He was thrilled.

I'd read in a book once at Pet Food Express that dogs roll in poop because they think it makes them smell

better to the opposite sex. True to form, after Gideon got up, he pranced around smelling of intestinal waste; his version of Old Spice. I fussed. I ran after him — but what for? The deed was done. "That's ok," I shouted, "you are getting hosed off before you get in the car Mister!" Peggy looked at me like "who's car are either of you getting into?" I was equal parts angry and embarrassed.

Rolling in poop had been something that I thought was a part of Gideon's puppy past — but it was lifting its ugly head again at a most inopportune time. Previously, I caught him rolling in the grass but it was usually where something *once was* if you get my drift. He had stopped eating poop as well as rolling in the real deal. I had firmly discouraged even rolling in the places where it once was... but on this Monday morning it was too late to fuss, the deed was done.

I started hosing Gideon down before I realized that I didn't have anything to dry him off. Urggh! Well, my hoody and pant leg was as good as anything else right? This is truly the fine print on the Mommy contract! Peggy is looking at me like my dog and I are about to get tied to a luggage rack to get back home. Luckily a man in the parking lot had a towel. I dried Gideon and thought "crisis averted." We all laughed it off and headed to the car when I realized that Gideon was not with the group. As I called to him I realized that this disappearance was standard issue when he was not ready to leave. I called and called to no avail. As I came back into the park from the parking lot he appeared. Did he come to his mommy? Nope. He went straight to the car filled parking lot. Luckily his aunt Peggy spotted him and screamed, "he's got boo boo on his face!" "What?" I said. "Gideon got boo boo on his face." As I approached, my funky butt dog ran to me — tongue flapping, eyes sparkling and poop shining on his left cheek. Urghh! Come here! Back to the hose. Back to the borrowed towel. Into the car.

As we rode home there was the awkward silence of "wow, I wish she had driven her own car," mixed with the jibes that come from the hilarity of being a dog owner and the realization that this smell had better wear off when we each bathe. As Gideon and I were dropped off and we parted from Peggy, Hope and JP, we laughed about the whole episode.

A thousand thoughts flood my mind about what it means to return to poop...

The scripture that comes to mind is Proverbs 26:11; "as a dog returns to his own vomit so a fool repeats his folly." Meaning — we often do not have the common sense not to repeat or go back to what was and still is refuse; waste; simplemindedness in our lives. Left to our own devices, we will behave just as Gideon did — we will go back and roll in poop, a behavior that should be a part of our past...

A flood of memories came to mind; times when I walked away from a bad relationship or toxic situation only to return to it again for some sack of ridiculous reasons that dissipate upon impact. How many of you have found yourselves returning to the poop? Doesn't even matter what exactly the poop is: a relationship, a job, a household; a mental, emotional or physical condition — poop is poop. It is not to be rolled in. It is not to be revisited. It is not to be smeared on us again especially not somebody else's — but when we go backward in our lives rather than forward we settle and we resign ourselves to wallow, roll or otherwise smear ourselves in something that is not even fit for grass, let alone for adornment.

Poop is only good for two things: for release and for the recycle bin. When you find yourself returning to poop, do exactly what I did for Gideon and for me: hose yourself off at the point of contact; go home, take a nice hot bath and deodorize. Then promise yourself that you will never, ever return to that stinky, smelly place again.

Be encouraged.

The Risk To Love

I don't like Pitt Bulls. Never have. As much as I LOVE dogs, I have always been a little afraid and a little wary. My neighbor got a Pitt Bull puppy — a sweet dog, but I could see the tendencies; a little too aggressive; slightly unpredictable and (drum roll) Gideon loved him! OMG. So I was just about to change my opinion when...

I was at a café in Berkeley and a Pitt Bull got loose from its owner and attacked a Pomeranian tied up out front. The amazed owners tried to separate the two: screaming, punching, pulling, begging — nothing worked. The jaw locked on the neck of the small dog and we all thought it was dead the way it was thrown and shaken, blood everywhere. I was so outraged; before I knew it I'd run outside and put my hands into the dog's mouth to try to dislodge this poor dog's neck from its clutches — also to no avail. Café patrons and passersby were traumatized by the whole episode. Days later I get an email with this subject line: THE POMERANIAN LIVED! Thank God.

Pitt Bulls are a popular breed in the Bay. I run into them on the street and at most dog parks off leash and unaltered with smiling owners saying that they're harmless. Yet the news betrays their assertion. In the last year alone there have been several maulings, the most recent, a pregnant woman killed in an attack by her own dog. While it is easy to say that these stories are exceptions, the fact still remains that this breed has got a *reputation*.

Then I move into a neighborhood where most of my neighbors have Pitt Bulls and there are strays. One day I came home to find a neighbor's pit on the sidewalk in front of my house — his ribs showing. I'd seen this dog before, emaciated and weak. I ran inside and before I knew it — I'd called him to me, fed him and given him cold water. Now, every time I see him, he approaches, tail wagging. So much for fear, something else kicked in. Today, I saw another loose Pitt Bull on the street having broken free from something by the looks of the harness dragging behind him. He too had protruding ribs, and almost walked in front of the car. I stopped and called to him but Gideon barked and he ran. Ironically I had food in the car so I followed him, calling to see if he'd come but he was fearful and confused. I drove ahead of him and put the food out. He approached, began eating and he lifted his head long enough for your eyes to meet. We were both smiling.

I learned yesterday that there's something stronger than fear... love. While Pitt Bulls are not my favorite breed, I never want to see any dog hurt or hungry or in trouble. Before I'd realized it, I had given this stray the food I borrowed for Gideon. I was struck by the impulse and reminded once again of the love of God toward us. God's love for us is not simply warm and fuzzy, it also ignores the risk. God's love will find us right where we are — *with a reputation*, lost, alone, confused and He will feed us, help us, encourage us; come see about us. I'm not God, don't get me wrong —but I sure do want to start behaving like God since I profess to be a Believer in Jesus Christ. Today, let's agree to be the love we want to see in the earth even when fear is the easier response. Remember, real love is a risk we take, no matter what the reputation, this is the love of God the world needs to see.

Be encouraged.

Epilogue

As the writing of this book came to a close, a series of events unfolded that really expanded the focus and intent of *Adventures In Gideon* going forward. In addition to this blog being a space to encouraged faith and good humor in the face of life's adventures and the full pursuit of the manifestation of the love of God christ it will also be a portal for pet adoption and rescue work.

There is a page on the website called Friends of Gideon that was reserved for the many canines and their humans that we encounter and come to know. That page will now be dedicated to the dogs we meet that need a home, or for whom we have successfully found a home. Our first rescue was a puppy I called *2lbs* who is now renamed *Possum*. She was found roaming near my church and ended up on my porch. I opened the door and there she was.She spent the night and the next morning we took her to the dog park and she was instantly adopted by Patsy, her husband and their Labradoodle, Gus. Our second rescue was Chulo, a 7 month old Chihuahua pup who was living with a family (two women, 1 cat, 1 Jack Russell Terrier) in Vallejo, stayed with me for 9 months and just found a forever home in Orinda. The third rescue is a white wire-haired dog I called Scrappy. Her name is now Vida and she is the official mascot of her new mommy's hair salon in Oakland and doing just fine. Then there was Lucky the pit-bull with the broken

leg. He wandered on my porch and it took me five days to get him into the car and to emergency vet services. Thankfully, Lucky was microchipped and was reunited with his owners. There has also been an addition to our clan, her name is Lily, a six-month old black Chihuahua pup and she is already turning the house upside down with endless hours of energy and play. Gideon loves her and she loves Gideon.

Finally, a new page will be added to the Adventures in Gideon website called Finding Grace. This page will be dedicated to the end of Pitt Bull fighting in Oakland and other urban centers. Grace was the name given to the most brutally attacked, yet sweetly trusting female Pitt Bull I've ever met. She was covered in puncture wounds; blood, urine and most of her jowl was missing when I found her tied to a pole in my church parking lot. Even with mortal wounds she allowed me to give her water; sing to her, read the bible to her and ultimately place her in the capable hands of the ones who would provide her medical care. I will never forget Grace's eyes nor will I forget her plight.

I invite everyone of God's intercessors to pray for the end of pit-bull fighting and the abuse of this breed for that purpose.

Here are some suggested prayer points:

- Supernatural investigative ability on the part of law enforcement

- The strong arm of the Lord to stand against the activity

- That God would visit each perpetrator

- That God would embolden those who hear and see suspicious activity to report it and that there would be no retaliation against them

- That none of these cruel people would ever be able to own any living thing until they are delivered/rehabilitated

- That dog fighters would be prosecuted to the fullest extent of the law

- That each Pitt Bull would be saved and placed in a loving, stable, fur-ever home

- That God would uproot and overturn this evil, murderous and cruel spirit operating in communities across the country.

The Adventure Continues